Begging the Question

by Sherwyn Jellico

From www.begthequestion.info:

"Begging the question" is a form of logical fallacy in which a statement or claim is assumed to be true without evidence other than the statement or claim itself. When one begs the question, the initial assumption of a statement is treated as already proven without any logic to show why the statement is true in the first place.

Begging the Question
Copyright © 2017 Sherwyn Jellico
Paperback edition
Written and edited by Sherwyn Jellico
Cover design by Sherwyn Jellico
Published by Jelli Baby Publishing
ISBN: 978-1-9997883-1-5

The right of Sherwyn Jellico to be identified as the author of this work has been asserted by him in accordance with the Copyright, Designs and Patents Act 1988.

All rights reserved. No part of this book may be reproduced, stored in a retrieval system, or transmitted in any form or by any means, without the prior written permission of the author. You must not circulate this book in any format.

Every effort has been made to fulfil requirements with regard to reproducing copyright material. The author will be glad to rectify any omissions at the earliest opportunity.

Disclaimer: While every precaution has been taken during the preparation of the book, neither the author nor Jelli Baby Publishing shall have any liability to any person or entity with respect to any loss or damage caused or alleged to be caused directly or indirectly by the use or misuse of the information contained in this book. There is absolutely no assurance that any statement contained within this book is true, accurate, complete or current. The author is not qualified in medicine, psychotherapy or pharmacology. The information provided in this book is no more than the author's personal opinion and unqualified conjecture. It should not under any circumstances be taken as a substitute for advice from a qualified doctor. If you think you may have OCD or depression, then you should seek a diagnosis and advice about treatment from a qualified doctor.

For all my oblivious brothers and sisters,
still out there in the badlands,
wandering in circles,
thirsting for certainty,
feeling completely alone.

This book is for you.

You are not alone.

Contents

Introduction

Welcome to my collection of poems about obsessive compulsive disorder(OCD) and depression. These are unusual conditions and my journey with them has been a tortuous one. As such, I could happily make this introduction last the entire length of the book. But this is first and foremost a poetry book, so I wanted to keep the introduction reasonably succinct. To that end, I've included four appendices at the back of the book to expand upon certain subjects briefly touched on here in the introduction. That way, it's up to the reader whether to get straight into the poems after this brief preamble, or whether to learn a bit more about those subjects first. While the appendices aren't a prerequisite for reading the poems, they might just help put a few things in context. If you're new to OCD, then I'd at least recommend reading the appendix about OCD before reading the poems.

Please see Appendix 1 for more information about OCD.

I want to make it absolutely clear at the outset, that I'm not qualified in medicine, psychotherapy or pharmacology. I'm just an ordinary man giving a voice to his experience of things he barely understands himself. The poems were written at different times and reflect a whole range of vacillating moods and ideas. No doubt there are contrasting extremes and contradictions along the way. This book is neither intended as a text book nor a self-help guide. It's just a poetry book with some supporting information. That information amounts to no more than a layman's conjecture which could be misleading or wrong. Never intentionally of course, but it's always a risk when an unqualified person discusses such slippery subjects. I strongly advise against forming any opinions about OCD, depression, therapy or medication based on anything I've written in this book. If you'd like to learn more about these subjects, then I'd urge you to seek out some recommended books written by qualified experts instead. Unlike me, they will be subject to peer review and scrutiny. After reading those books, you may well conclude that I'm talking out of my hat here.

I started writing poems about these conditions four years ago, after the mind-blowing revelation that I'd been obliviously living with OCD for the last thirty years of my life; first undiagnosed for thirteen years, and then misdiagnosed as clinical depression. Prior to this late epiphany, I was living in limbo for the longest time. With no idea what my mystery problem was, I was eventually driven to the conclusion that I was either cursed or had a unique mental illness which defied modern medicine.

Once I knew it wasn't just me, and I didn't have to hide my hideous secret any more, it felt natural to open up about it. An OCD charity was asking for poems about the disorder to display on their website, so I decided to have a go at writing one. I'd hardly written any poetry before that, but I found it to be an effective form of alchemy for expressing what I'd been through. Well, my poor old poem didn't make the final cut, but I was already hooked so I carried on writing poetry regardless. It was only in intermittent trickles at first, but once I found my sea legs a year or two later, an unstoppable tsunami followed.

There's a reason it took me so long to work out that I had OCD. The bulk of my symptoms fall under the heading of *pure O*. This is a less publicised form of OCD, characterised by mental rituals, in notable contrast to the physical rituals normally associated with OCD. I would guess that OCD first came onto my radar some time in the 1990s, but I didn't find out about pure O until I stumbled on it quite by accident four years ago.

Please see Appendix 1 for more information on pure O, and Appendix 2 for more about my journey with OCD.

I've suffered with depression all of my adult life. It's hard to say with any certainty which came first, OCD or depression. That said, it's very common for a diagnosis of depression to accompany OCD. Dealing with OCD around the clock grinds you down in no time, taking a toll on your quality of life, and leaving you feeling increasingly dejected and isolated.

Please see Appendix 3 for more information on depression.

The split of OCD/depression poems in this book is roughly fifty-fifty. I considered categorising the poems under different headings, but in the end I couldn't see much value in that. So instead I've tried to mix them all up so that there's some variety - a bit like a really miserable box of chocolates.

Some poems are more loosely associated with OCD or depression. Some discuss the inevitable withdrawal and isolation that goes hand-in-hand with these conditions. Some focus on the addictive aspects of OCD. Some are about the suicidal ideation which inevitably occurs when mental illness crashes up against overwhelming pressures and a lack of support. Some deal with the volatile nature of hope and despair in such circumstances. And some reflect my intense dislike of the assumptions projected onto OCD sufferers regarding therapy and medication.

Please see Appendix 4 for a discussion about these assumptions.

I've even sneaked in a couple of poems which aren't to do with OCD or depression at all, but hopefully it will become apparent why I've included them where I have.

While my OCD predominantly takes the form of pure O, I do have some physical compulsions too. It's seldom a clean split - people with pure O often have other aspects of OCD thrown into the mix, and vice versa. The OCD poems reflect this mix, with the majority focussing on pure O, but with some addressing those other aspects - e.g. Dear Ears covers dermatillomania(skin picking), and Nuts and Bolts is about repeatedly checking locks and switches.

I wanted to include all the necessary colours to paint the fullest picture I could, and make no mistake, it's not a pretty picture. These are dark subjects indeed. I'm going out of my way here to surgically focus on the worst aspects of OCD and depression as I've experienced them. So maybe don't leave this one on the coffee table for the kids to stumble on and flick through after school.

Please understand though that this is not the whole picture of me. I don't go around with a head full of this stuff all the time. I have days where these problems settle more into the background and life takes on a brighter complexion. I exercise, I laugh, I play, I talk nonsense, I sing in the shower, I do chores, I do childish things. Hell, I've even been known to leave the house on occasion and visit the art gallery. I try wherever possible to be positive and defy the workings of a treacherous mind to accomplish good things. Oh, and I do write poems about all manner of other things too.

Some poems span more than one page. I decided not to break verses across pages, so occasionally there's a gap at the bottom of a page before the poem continues on the next page. Whenever poems carry over to the next page, you will find 3 dots on the bottom right of the page, like this: ...

Some of the pieces I've chosen to include in this book - e.g. Supermarket OCD Avalanche, Reverse Engineering Mega-Doubt, and The Gauntlet - are somewhat sprawling and lacking in any real structure. I decided to include them regardless, because I believe that they convey my experience of OCD better than anything else I've written. Likewise with more structured but long and repetitive pieces - e.g. Where's the Off Switch Again and Sisyphus. The laboured repetition in these poems is meant to bludgeon the reader into resentful dizzy submission; echoing the endless repetition imposed on sufferers by OCD. That said, the poem would have to stretch to about a million pages to accurately capture that, and I didn't think people would make it to the end if I was that faithful to the subject in hand.

I contemplated playing it safe, and replacing all of the swear words in my poems with more innocuous words instead. But every time I went to replace them, it just did not sit right with me somehow. It felt like a betrayal of the original spirit of the poem, and a disservice to what I originally set out to do here. In the end I realised that I'd used those precise words for good reason. i.e. the cumulative frustration and anger that OCD leaves me with, often has me swearing like a trooper. Perhaps it's a necessary cathartic outlet, like a radiator letting off steam. Better that than some act of violence or self-harm surely? So after much thought, I decided it's only right that this is accurately reflected in the poems. Otherwise, what's the point of this book? A watered-down version of OCD and depression to please the crowd? Not in this life! After what I've been through, I'm going to tell it how it is.

I've also used pejorative terms like "loony" in some poems. I want to make it absolutely clear that these words are used either as self-deprecating humour, or as my perception of an imaginary outsider's perspective. I'd never use such terms in a malicious or disrespectful way towards my fellow sufferers. Frankly, they've been through quite enough already. Besides, it would be a bizarrely self-defeating gesture.

I do however understand that some people have strong views about such things, and if any of the language I've used in this book offends anybody, then I apologise for that. That said, I do think it's vital that we find humour in this thing wherever we can. It's too damned hard and painful otherwise. At some of my lowest points, I've found it remarkably liberating to see the dark humour or absurdity in the situation; to defy the torment with counter-intuitive laughter. To be fair though, it's rare that you can do that when you're trapped with looping anxiety ramped up through the roof. But if you can somehow pull it off, it's a free gift to yourself that takes a lot of power away from the aggressor.

Talking of the aggressor, it's interesting how we OCD sufferers tend to externalise our disorder into some malevolent outside entity. When you're on the receiving end though, it really does feel like something or someone external is sabotaging your life; tripping you up when you least expect it; laying land mines to catch you out and humiliate you. In reality of course, it's all just the product of our own minds. Nevertheless, this externalisation does seem to help when discussing OCD, and sometimes even therapists will personify OCD to get a point across. As such, I sometimes personify OCD as the Devil or some other evil entity in my poems.

Likewise, there are references to God in some of my poems. Now, I don't subscribe to man-made religions. So for me, God is a catch-all for the living cosmos and whatever lies behind it. While I've genuinely no wish to denigrate anyone else's religious beliefs, I'm not personally convinced that man-made religions describe that very well. Alternatively, I might use God and the Devil in poems to represent the good and bad forces at work in my own mind; my better and worse angels so to speak. The poem I-con touches on this subject.

So why write a book of poems focusing solely on OCD and depression anyway? I'm awfully glad you asked me that. Well, I think I wrote it for three reasons:

- Firstly, and most simply, to resonate with fellow sufferers. Emancipation from thirty years of hard OCD time in solitary confinement, seems to have left me with the overwhelming urge to stand up and bear witness. Not so much in the sense of "I said hallelujah! Praise the LORD!" but more in the sense of "Say, isn't it annoying when you get interrupted in the middle of a compulsion?".

- Secondly, to spread the word. There's been an awful lot of misinformation in the media about OCD. As a result, you get some bizarre reactions when you tell people you've got it(see the poem Begging the Question for some examples). So I hope this book might give some non-sufferers a little window into a shrouded world that must be incredibly difficult to grasp without experiencing it first-hand. By shining a light into the darkest corners of my life, hopefully I can show people what it's like to live with pure O OCD and depression.

- Thirdly, and finally, in hope that somebody who's unaware they have OCD stumbles on this book by accident, and has the same kind of epiphany I had four years ago. Maybe eerie bells will start ringing as they read through the poems. Maybe they'll realise that they're not alone after all, and that their mystery problem is in fact OCD. Perhaps that's a little ambitious, but I can dream.

Please take this book as it's intended - not a self-help guide or a text book, but a poetry book; a travelogue charting one man's journey down one of life's more peculiar and less travelled roads. Thank you so much for picking up my book, and I really hope that you get a kick out of some of my poems.

p.s. OK, OK, OK - I was lying about the art gallery. I meant the chip shop really. I was trying to sound sophisticated. This godforsaken scrupulosity will be the end of me!

Poems

<u>Phineus</u>

The Devil sits there scheming on his perch,

he weighs up all the angles where I'm weak,

he dangles down his question mark to search,

for places where the meaning feels oblique.

His hound lifts up my skullcap with a hook,

exposing all that's going on inside,

to let his master get a better look,

so he can see where doubt is best applied.

He plants his rancid seed and it begins,

I pause and place my head inside my hands,

to make propitiations for my sins,

to jump through rings of fire like he commands.

He comes to see me many times a day,

it's like a holy rite I must perform,

to keep the lies and opposites at bay,

to save the quiet centre of my storm.

<u>We Face Away</u>

We face away,

when pointed things stick painful in our day.

We face away,

when scary monsters come around to play.

We face away,

when better angels fail to have their say.

We face away,

when mirrors crack and fragments go astray.

We face away,

when sights not fit for eyes are on display.

We face away.

Dark Collage

I drag around a dark collage,
of jagged glass and toxic rags.
I made it in self-sabotage,
my castle flies the worst of flags.

Should I forget my rightful place,
it slithers up and bids me look,
while spewing falsehoods in my face,
to make me bite the baited hook.

Beguiling me to stop and stare,
but staring stirs my hand to touch,
to right the wrongs it brings to bear,
which works but hurts my hand so much.

The fixing makes it taunt me more,
with sharper shards and fouler cloth.
I can't abide what I abhor,
lured onto candles like a moth.

...

It feels like death to look away,

but something's been revealed to me:

that when I choose to disobey,

it weakens its authority.

If I can just resist enough,

the glass begins to lose its bite,

the rags degrade to harmless fluff,

no more to blight my line of sight.

The collage never disappears,

it's like a test I sit each day,

reminding me my doubts and fears,

must be endured, not put away.

Double-Star-Crossed

God blew a kiss to Romeo,

and skewered needles through his brain.

Not even Juliet could sew,

his broken mind back up again.

He watched her dangled to and fro,

and fumbled clumsy for the prize,

but he knew one day she would go,

and leave him there with leaky eyes.

When that day came, all time stood still,

the bullet blew his world apart.

One shot, but what a tidy kill,

it took the last piece of his heart.

So now he wanders through the woods,

his lovers are the browns and greens.

No more he floats among the coulds,

but flogs himself with could've-beens.

A Tidal Mind

Buffeted by fickle tides
of terror and relief,
nursing razor blade insides
cut open on the reef.

Struggling to get on my feet
and stagger up the sand,
trouble if I don't complete
those castles that I planned.

Even if I beat the waves
and make it back to shore,
all I find are shallow graves,
no castles any more.

Desecration

There once was a peg who started out fine,
a curio carved from wood seldom grown.
The rest of the pegs abhorred God's design,
aghast at a shape at odds with their own.

They lured him down holes he just didn't fit,
then bludgeoned him through with blame and reward.
When something broke off, they sanded the split,
enamelled it over, and called him restored.

With all of the knocks, his shape has gone wrong,
he tries to fill holes, but can't touch the sides.
He wants to fit in, but doesn't belong.
You don't second-guess the shape God provides.

<u>Mantra</u>

Repeat the words you need to hear,

to quarantine the thing you fear,

to separate the truth and doubt,

and kick the uninvited out.

Repeat the words you need to hear,

whenever would-be thieves are near,

it's vital they don't get inside,

so in my mantras I abide.

Repeat the words you need to hear,

to make the monsters disappear,

but magic spells must be rehearsed,

as they don't always work at first.

Repeat the words you need to hear,

keep going till the coast is clear,

hang in there till you wear it down,

you crazy windmill tilting clown.

...

Repeat the words you need to hear,

to neutralise the bad idea,

but say it right with no mistakes,

or else the sleeping brood awakes.

<u>Moratorium</u>

Trying to remember how it felt ...

when the starch would melt away,

looking forward to a day,

drifting off without a care,

to really want to go somewhere,

to lose myself away from blame,

not feeling like I must explain,

not always caring for the others,

the times your heart sang with another's,

when people properly connect,

just to be treated with respect,

to do activities for fun,

to feel like it was me who won.

But I'll be damned if I will borrow,

what's just snatched away tomorrow.

So I fight the urge to cling,

to random flotsam fortune brings.

...

26

Watching loaded logs float by,

letting sleeping cogs lie,

as time grows shorter,

treading water.

Strings so long unstroked,

no longer ache,

for sounds they forgot how to make,

since the violin broke.

Echo Judo

When troubles break upon these rocks,

new waves appear and surge away.

They bounce around in aftershocks,

to re-emerge another day.

The ripples run and so it goes,

what's done is done, and not to do.

Don't try to change how water flows,

just step aside and let it through.

I Guess I Just Don't See the World That Way

The faithful get down on their knees and pray,

God helps those who can find the words to say,

don't ask cos there's no answers anyway,

I guess I just don't see the world that way.

I look at all the games you people play,

you work all day and sleep your nights away,

look forward to your summer holiday,

I guess I just don't see the world your way.

I try to make bright bubbles in my grey,

keep all my ugly opposites at bay,

crawl forward through my darkness come what may,

be thankful you don't see the world my way.

Cease the Day

The garden pirates make a din,
roll over, put some ear plugs in.
I got so tired of counting sheep,
now I count doubts to get to sleep.

The clock cries at the time I set,
I'd rise but I ain't ready yet.
Expecting me to wake is rude,
when I'm in such a rancid mood.

I'm gonna lie here till I feel,
like things are on an even keel.
Until then you can keep your day,
it's wasted on me anyway.

Twenty-Four Carrot Cruelty

I'm tired of meeting lovely women,
there's hundreds in the town I live in,
like lettuce left to mock the rabbit,
whose jaws are locked so he can't grab it.

It feels like nature knows I'm broken,
it limits me with laws unspoken,
it makes them look with sideways glances,
and ends my reproductive chances.

I get it, but it makes me wonder,
why I should pay for nature's blunder,
such pointless pain left unanointed,
forgive me if I'm disappointed.

Missing Information

I call it doubt.

It's a catchall.

To call it that, is to misunderstand the problem;

like calling a sunflower "soil" in winter.

Soil is the ending, not the whole story.

This thing doesn't start with doubt.

This thing starts with missing information.

Imagine making a very important meal.

You go to the pantry to grab that fusilli pasta you bought yesterday...

… only it's not there any more.

You're the only one who uses the pantry.

You know deep down that you bought that pasta.

You were there in the shop and everything.

You have no history of delusions.

Yet somehow against all reason,

now that you need it,

it's gone.

And it wouldn't matter,

but this is a really important meal.

…

It means a lot to you.

You can't just say "Never mind!",

and put it down to experience.

You're not going to crack open a can of beans and forget about it.

So you put your life on hold,

and keep going back to check.

The pantry light seems to have stopped working,

so you take your best torch.

You strain beyond your natural limits,

to peer into every crevice of the pantry,

to scrutinise every single item.

You figure if you go back enough times,

and try enough different strategies,

eventually you will locate the missing pasta ...

... and so it goes,

around and round,

down and down,

until you drive yourself insane.

...

You cannot stop checking now.

Yet, every time you check,

by virtue of some black magic you'll never understand,

it only makes your pasta questions intensify and multiply.

Enter doubt.

If you can't be sure about the pasta,

then how can you ever be sure about anything else in the pantry?

Maybe it wasn't fusilli – maybe it was penne?

Maybe you didn't even buy the pasta in the first place?

Maybe you're not even into pasta?

Maybe you're more a rice kind of guy?

Yes that must be it.

You wouldn't be having these unassailable doubts otherwise.

Why don't you just give up and accept what you really are?

Dirty rice boy!

...

Slowly,

slowly,

catchy monkey,

in the Chinese finger trap.

<u>Nil by Mouth</u>

He's nil by mouth,

he goes without,

for he is touched,

his mind went South.

No friends as such,

he's not allowed.

Best walk around,

or don't go out,

until the touched

one's not about.

Always Be Resisting

Interminable gifts,
worst possible what ifs,
holes you'd fit your fist in,
... always be resisting.

Nefarious notions,
stirring placid oceans,
tranquil currents twisting,
... always be resisting.

The Devil's seed of doubt,
flips fears inside out,
question marks persisting,
... always be resisting.

Pigeon Hole

Artificial pigeon hole,
a trick of modern politics,
surreptitious mind control,
to sucker all the lunatics.

When a person doesn't fit,
inside the box you need 'em to,
stick a false box onto it,
cajole 'em in, and kick 'em through.

Oppressive Convulsive Debaucher

I set myself a million tests a day.

Good news - I passed them all today. Hooray!

I have to though cos failing,

means my opposites prevailing,

and I'm not prepared to lose this war that way.

But none of them can know about my secret skill,

to see the hidden links and bend them to my will,

and little do they know,

that when I switch out of their flow,

it's demons who would harm us that I kill.

Things they dismiss as disconnected,

we with the gift see intersected.

God forbid that anyone imply

we should try to walk on by,

leaving the unacceptable uncorrected.

Then all the wrong things get infected.

Like extra verses where they don't belong!

Curses invoked by thinking something wrong,

a word planted by the Devil in a song,

to trip us up, and flip us into what we dreaded all along.

...

It's all lies and I can see that clearly now,

just got to make it stick this time and not allow,

my mind to shake up like an Etch A Sketch,

but when I go back later to check I betcha,

it'll all be washed away again somehow.

It always is.

Same old doubts fizz through my walls,

to kick me squarely in the balls,

and leave me back at square one,

all my new resolve gone.

I need a rest before I can carry on this time.

<u>On the Turn</u>

To whom it may concern,

these days I'm feeling kinda strange.

My life is on the turn,

somehow the taste of it has changed.

What used to be in bloom,

is now beginning to recede,

encumbered and consumed,

by creeping bramble bush and weed.

Sweet fancies I once had,

about the way my life might be,

have one-by-one gone bad,

and decomposed in front of me.

When sweet gives way to sour,

when all your dreams are laid to waste,

what looked so good an hour

ago, now leaves a bitter taste.

<u>Cuckolded</u>

The Devil made me cuckold yesterday.
The jealousy is more than I can stand.
He ran off with my mind and had his way.
It felt as though he had the whole thing planned.

I'd like to say it only happened once,
but saying that would sadly be a lie.
He often calls and takes her out to lunch,
as regular as tea and apple pie.

My mind and I, we still put up a fight,
refusing just to cower and obey.
Yet still he steals her off into the night,
and rides her till he's had his wicked way.

<u>Off Switch</u>

Some days I wish I had a secret switch,

a shotgun or a potion from a witch,

a safety net in case,

I fall too far back in the race,

or for those times when life's just too much of a bitch.

Regret and guilt can get too much to bear,

an open wound that simply won't repair,

too much to heave round,

with unshod feet on burning ground,

cos life chewed up the only shoes I had to wear.

Should that far off horizon start to swell,

with thunder clouds that do not mean me well,

I'll feel less terrified,

if I've an off switch by my side,

safe in the knowledge that I won't be trapped in Hell.

The Ill-Mannered Guest

A stranger keeps on knocking and protesting at my door,

I should just leave him hanging cos I've seen it all before,

but he wears these clever masks,

he demands and never asks,

and he talks my better judgement down into the bottom drawer.

When he walks in I ask him to remove his muddy shoes,

but I should know by now that my request will be refused.

As if that's not enough,

he treads in horrid stuff,

and he stomps it with a smile into my carpet's sunken hues.

The optimist in me believes he's capable of change,

I try to coax him into a more sensible exchange,

but he just stands there knowing,

exactly where it's going,

impervious as he weighs up what mischief is in range.

I find myself incapable of being a nasty host,

I seat him in the living room and make him tea and toast.

He swipes it from my hands,

picks up the bread and jam,

and smears it on the things he knows will make me hurt the most.

...

The photos of my family lie strewn about and smashed,

he's given Auntie Margaret a comedy moustache.

He made my little niece,

look cross-eyed and obese,

and where my grandad's portrait was there's just a pile of ash.

He works his way from room to room degrading all that's dear,

I try to calm him down and whisper reason in his ear,

but he stays until he's finished,

till my peace of mind's diminished,

till I'm crouching in the corner rocking back and forth in fear.

He leaves and I recover and I get the place detoxed,

I take some new precautions like replacing all the locks,

fit cameras outside,

build a moat a mile wide,

but lately it occurs to me, it's only friends it blocks.

And Then It Falls Apart

Somehow the usual adornments and distractions

have worn thin again,

just evaporated away without warning,

leaving a terrible new version of the world,

without any of the familiar consolations,

without anything to grab onto.

Everything too far away or cold to the touch,

mocking you with new colours not fit for eyes;

a stark version of your life,

without the fairy tales,

without hope or happy endings;

the accurate version,

that the circus of bullshit normally stifles.

But it looks like the circus left town in the night,

and now you're pinned down and forced to face the truth;

the crushing inescapable truth,

that feels like it cannot be borne another day.

...

And the only thing stopping you switching it off,

is the fear something worse will replace it,

because you wouldn't put it past a god,

who was capable of making a world,

where feeling like this for no reason

was possible.

<u>The Spinners</u>

We dash around from pole to pole,
to keep our babies spinning round.
We're terrified we'll lose control,
and hear that dreaded smashing sound.

The reasons why, we can't recall,
it doesn't matter anyway.
Keep spinning so the plates don't fall,
cos otherwise there's hell to pay.

<u>Ballast</u>

Someone open my heart,
let the heaviness out,
blow the levee apart,
put an end to this drought.

I don't want it to stop,
not until it's all purged,
fetch a bucket and mop,
lest we end up submerged.

Maybe then I can fly,
without carrying care,
like a hawk in the sky,
soaring lighter than air.

Quid Pro Quo

A murderous triffid with poisonous spores,

a flesh-eating zombie who's covered in sores,

a cobra with wings and extendable jaws,

a horseman whose head was cut off in the wars,

a hook-handed pirate who walks through closed doors,

a dog with three heads skulking round on all fours,

a fiend in my mind fixed on finding my flaws,

a sudden attack with no obvious cause,

a festering wound ripped back open with claws,

reliving my fears in a punitive pause,

abhorrent ideas my conscience abhors,

vile lies dressed as truth to the Devil's applause,

I'll show you my monsters if you show me yours.

How to Deal with the Udders

Baulk at things which feel uneven,
back away from forced agreement.
This one's mind seems kinda tricksy,
get him down the doctor's quickly.

No attempt to understand it,
wonder drugs dreamt up and branded,
doctors dodge the diagnosis,
pick the pills that match it closest.

Why waste time confronting demons?
Put away those funny feelings,
switch them off with good narcotics,
flood the brain and plug the sockets.

Peddlers backed by institutions,
pushing packaged pill solutions,
doctors selling out their calling,
numbed till you forget you're falling.

...

Side effects are known to vary:
hope you like your nightmares scary,
bye bye hard-on, bye bye weeping,
swollen tongues and screwed up sleeping.

Lab to box to doctors office,
legion leeches pocket profits,
punters hooked on pills and sessions,
keeps a leech in nice possessions.

Blind us all with pseudoscience,
presuppose complete compliance,
do away with dialectics,
close it down and call us sceptics.

Under served by overseers,
care and welfare disappears,
orphaned off to join the circus,
serving private healthcare's purpose.

Cavalier with regulations,
unafraid of allegations,
greasing palms of regulators,
out of reach of alligators.   ...

Wait until you hear the sequel,

peddlers always need new people,

running out of gents and ladies,

now they want your kids and babies.

<u>My Stupid Stupid Stupid Brain</u>

Sometimes my brain throws me a no when I mean yes,
it leads to elevated stress,
I have to clean up all the mess.

Sometimes my brain says I meant this when I meant that,
I ask for dog, it gives me cat,
it breaks my heart, the little brat.

Sometimes my brain tells me I like the things I hate,
it tries to sneak them through the gate,
I must not let them infiltrate.

Sometimes my brain forgets the thing that I just saw,
like whether I just locked the door,
so I go back and check once more.

Sometimes my brain can't grasp a word or an idea,
the lights are on but no one's here,
so I repeat until it's clear.

Sometimes my brain catastrophises the what-ifs,
behemoth battles born from tiffs,
a mind in shackles shies from risks.   ...

Sometimes my brain goes to the left when I go right,

we disagree all day and night,

I'd rather die than lose this fight.

<u>Reality Check</u>

Christ how the hell'd it get to this?
Just letting go is precious bliss,
but getting there outweighs the hit,
eight thousand times and then a bit.

I wonder how it came to pass,
the boy who tried so hard in class,
could reach the bottom of the pile,
it's frightful hard to reconcile.

If this was chess then I'd concede,
my king is in a mess indeed,
he's running out of squares to tread,
the crown is slipping off his head.

I'm running on thin air these days,
bamboozled by these modern ways,
I can't act how they tell me to,
I always seem to miss my cue.

...

As I ride out these final years,

in free fall, changing down the gears,

there's one thought I cannot dismiss:

Christ how the hell'd it get to this?

Doubt Puppet

Commanded by my doubt,
it wears me like a glove.
It makes me dance about,
controlling from above.

I'm frightened to refuse,
to cut away the strings.
Are birds allowed to lose,
the feathers from their wings?

Instead I just obey,
I dance until I'm sore,
and once it's had its way,
it throws me on the floor.

I dream of breaking free,
of roaming unattached,
of dancing just for me,
the puppeteer dispatched.

<u>Falling</u>

I watch the grains of sand fall through,
and wonder what it's all about.
Accusers cloud my rear view,
they know my time is running out.

Water Wheel

When people ask what's wrong with me,

I baulk at saying OCD,

they act like it's a fallacy,

they only weigh up what they see.

They think it's all these things it's not,

like people washing hands a lot,

or fussing with the things they've got,

but mine's like mental Mandelbrot.

Don't get me wrong, it can be those,

but thorns alone don't make a rose,

without the doubt no garden grows,

well mine comes from a fireman's hose.

I gulp it down in bucket loads,

to dull the taste from licking toads.

but then it floods my winding roads,

which swell up till my mind explodes.

...

If only I could make you feel,

the awfulness of this ordeal,

revolving on a water wheel,

re-drowned and brought around to heal.

Pray listen while I make it clear,

that even though some quirks appear,

the underlying problem here,

is doubt ramped through the stratosphere.

<u>Off My Trolley</u>

Hey God I want a refund,

on this crap defective brain.

It won't respond to treatment,

it just carries on the same.

You put my prayers on answer,

and you won't return my calls,

you're like a Cossack dancer,

sent to kick me in the balls.

Well when this life has finished,

me and you are gonna talk.

I'll down a tin of spinach,

and I'll stab you with a fork.

You've given me the trolley,

with the wheel that doesn't work,

a brain by Stan and Ollie,

on a trek like Captain Kirk.

...

Some day they might start growing,

new replacement brains and more.

Till then I'm boldly going,

where no man has gone before.

Redoubt

Ride a bike that has no wheels.

Rush your meals.

One way deals.

Could this be how madness feels?

Best laid mines of mice and men.

Not again.

Goodbye Zen.

Trod on one with my size ten.

Bad news from the recon scout:

"Wolves about!".

"Roger, out".

Back behind the walled redoubt.

Secondary Gains

Secondary gains:

whereby an opportunist frames,

your wood that goes against their grain,

as down to problems in your brain.

Folks are strange that way,

they like to censor what you say,

to shape events like potter's clay,

they look for leverage all day.

Trouble is with that,

it's going to end up tit-for-tat,

I'll use it when I'm feeling trapped,

an ace I keep beneath my hat.

Golden get-out clause,

invoked to get me out of chores,

to shirk my duties so they're yours,

that's how it goes with two-way doors.

Pain Stopped Play

Neurons in rebellion,

over twenty billion.

Plenty of good reasons

not to leave the home pavilion.

Bowler's got a paddy on,

ball's made from plutonium.

Lighting up the outfield

with a yield of thirteen kilotons.

One-oh-one Orwellian,

scared to put the telly on.

Make them come inside so

I can bite them back and bury them.

Can't take more delirium,

warm up the DeLorean.

Back to Roman Times to

bag a cohort of Praetorians.

...

Bring back five battalions,

cavalry on stallions.

Round my head they'll prance and

run their lances through rapscallions.

Sick of picking carrion,

turning vegetarian.

From now on I get my

food from orchards or aquariums.

<u>Holoboulos</u>

I keep finding I'm stuck down a hole,
then my life is consumed with escape.
Once I climb out and vanquish my goal,
I resume life in much better shape.

But it still feels like something's not right,
and I start to lose grip on control,
dropping down to my knees at the sight,
as it hits me I'm in a new hole.

The Mock Chess Monster

I lost a game of chess today.

I lost the same game yesterday.

It really feels like I can win,

but then the fun and games begin.

My foe is trained in arcane arts,

manipulating minds and hearts,

he lets you think you stand a chance,

then leads you on a merry dance.

The squares distort, the colours change,

the knights and rooks all rearrange,

the rules get wrestled out of whack,

my king dies from a heart attack.

It doesn't matter how I play,

I end up losing anyway.

He taints the game so he can't lose,

he paints my brain in blacks and blues.

...

I've had enough of guilt and blame,

I need to find another game.

It's harmful to my mental health,

to lose at chess against myself.

<u>The Impostor</u>

I ought to get an honorary Oscar,
a lifetime recognition type award,
to celebrate my role as an imposter,
a fabricator perpetrating fraud.

I studied at the method school of acting,
I have to get immersed inside my role,
the standards that I strive for are exacting,
convincing them I'm normal is my goal.

It's hard to stay in character forever,
a subtle kind of subterfuge I wield,
with feats of misdirection I endeavour,
to keep my true identity concealed.

But if you linger long enough you're certain,
to spot the real me between the cracks,
you're guaranteed a glimpse behind the curtain,
whenever I'm unsure or I relax.

<u>Pimp My Pride</u>

I'm pissed off with my therapist,
she's just a grubby middle man,
who shifts stuff for the pharmacist,
like sertraline and Ativan.

I'm pissed off with my therapist,
the talking part is just a sham,
I told her no but she insists,
that I should take citalopram.

I'm pissed off with my therapist,
she's like a broken record now,
she cherry-picks for things to twist,
to make me milk big pharma's cow.

I'm pissed off with my therapist,
I told her pills are not a cure,
the proper problem ends up missed,
and covered up in cow manure.

...

I'm pissed off with my therapist,

she's selling out the British youth,

a subsidised apologist,

for those who'd seek to mask the truth.

<u>In a Pickle</u>

I'm hooked on squeezing lemons,

day and night, it's like my penance.

Just one more will see me right,

I'll close the door and lock it tight.

Then I can get on with my life ...

Then there's this itch, this little tickle,

then the pictures start to trickle,

and I'm piggy in the middle,

of the have-to and the fickle.

In the throes of pain and pleasure,

highs and lows in equal measure.

It's a self-fulfilling riddle,

when you're followed by a feather.

Lost boys beg me to untether

them, to run back home to Neverland.

I wonder if I'll ever

wriggle out of this damn pickle jar.

The world I fell from seems so far away.

<u>Where's the Off Switch Again?</u>

Counting candles,

stepping stone,

how much further on my own?

Exes echo,

wonder why,

always winds up with goodbye.

Toxic taxi,

chewed-up cheek,

tired of playing hide and seek.

Assam addict,

taking tea,

punctuates banality.

Broaching breakfast,

eggs again,

poach a foetus from a hen.

Bulging belly,

absent abs,

crunches are for eating crabs.   ...

Matching metre,

rhyme rehearsed,

work the words into a verse.

Sickly syrup,

drip-fed dross,

comfort feeds on reason's loss.

Circus surplus,

clumsy clown,

dancing with his trousers down.

Languid linguist,

tangled tongue,

plucking strings too highly strung.

Forcing faces,

masking mood,

strap a smile on when you're nude.

Loaded ladder,

treacle trail,

tortoise overtakes the snail.

...

Jaded judgement,

trampled trust,

mangled in the cut and thrust.

Pre-empt problems,

hollow hope,

pragmatist or misanthrope?

Dreading drama,

bound to bite,

can't accept what isn't right.

Squawkers squabbling,

wobbling wits,

quarrels leave my mind in bits.

Spitfire spirit,

Templar type,

undercooked and overripe.

Constant conflict,

rushed reload,

scuppered by this honour code.

...

Conscience cancer,

treason trap,

can't buy dinner with a clap.

Legal Lego,

building blocks,

box in the unorthodox.

Talking turkey,

turgid terms,

wonder how much this chick earns?

Milking moments,

wrestling right,

meaning keeps me up all night.

Boxing bullshit,

ducking doubt,

fighting fires to put them out.

Juggling jigsaws,

solving self,

puzzled by my mental health.

...

Steady stifle,

trickling ticks,

life in dread of spinning sticks.

Surfing circles,

looping life,

stuck in self-fulfilling strife.

Turn off torment,

weigh up ways,

tourniquet these troubled days.

Purpose private,

hidden here,

test conditions make that clear.

Absent answers,

phone a friend,

they won't know though some pretend.

Fruit forbidden,

never nice,

deities don't play with dice.

...

Drowsy dreamtime,

quantum quilt,

in a cot that tricksters built.

Quest for questions,

why and when,

if there's no God ... well what then?

<u>Learning</u>

Learning my mind's the kinda place a bad idea grows.

Learning the bad ideas are never what I suppose.

Learning to dance with myself without treading on my toes.

<u>Quarantine</u>

I don't seem to be what they need me to be,
revelation from trial and error.
I tried to become it but faltered you see,
with a mind half-inclined towards terror.

Until some redeemer expunges this curse,
I will keep myself out of the running.
I'll make would-be lovers recoil and disperse,
with strange feats of self-sabotage cunning.

To live out my days in a Templar regime,
as a warrior monk on a mission.
Maintaining my heart under strict quarantine,
while I quest for my grail's apparition.

Begging the Question

You need to get yourself to the doctor and get some medication.

Have you tried transcendental meditation?

Have you thought about medication?

It's like arranging pens and washing hands loads isn't it?

What medication are you on then?

Oh yeah, I know, that thing the famous footballer's got.

Are you taking medication?

That cage-fighting champion's got the same thing as you, right?

Do you take some medication for that then?

We had a dog with that once - it was hilarious.

Why aren't you on medication?

My wife's got that - she's always arranging the towels and stuff.

Why aren't you on medication?

Oh yeah I had that once, but I just decided I wasn't gonna do it any more.

Why aren't you on medication?

Sure, I'm a little bit OCD too.

Why aren't you on medication?

Like, OMG, I'm sooooooooooo OCD.

Why aren't you on medication?

I bet your house is really spotless then, LOL.

Why aren't you on medication?

You know what you need - to join a nice rambling club.

Why aren't you on medication?   ...

You just need more confidence, that's your problem.

Why aren't you on medication?

Yeah but it's not a disability is it, more a quirk or a phase.

Why aren't you on medication?

We all just want what's best for you.

Why aren't you on medication?

Listen, I'm here to help people with serious health problems, and, well, yours isn't really is it?

Why aren't you on medication?

But if you think about those things, doesn't that mean you're into them on some level?

Why aren't you on medication?

It can be cured with a combination of SSRI medication and therapy.

Why aren't you on medication?

He coped with the assessment and didn't display any symptoms of anxiety throughout.

Why aren't you on medication?

He uses coping mechanisms to deal with his OCD and is therefore fit for work.

Why aren't you on medication?

That Sweater

That sweater in the sales,

that fell off the rack,

onto the floor.

Trod on,

kicked about,

strange marks,

misshapen and snagged.

Was probably alright yesterday,

but now everyone knows it's never getting sold,

no matter how many times they cross out the price,

and write a cheaper one under it.

No one bothers picking it up any more,

and putting it back on the rack,

not even the shop staff.

Best take that sweater out back and have it shot,

cos it's making the customers nervous.

<u>1UP</u>

Pursued around the same old maze,

I must evade the hungry ghosts.

They feast upon my doubtful ways,

the things I love and fear the most.

I feed off thoughts to fuel my flight,

the best ones let me bite them back.

Alas, it seems the more I bite,

the more it seems to bait the pack.

Whenever I survive the maze,

before I get to take a breath,

it starts again and writing says:

"Get ready - you've got one life left!".

Pyromaniac

My moth-like mind,

ill-inclined

to gnaw at the inane.

Blindly drawn,

towards whom or what

I find more fun,

or what will simply numb the pain.

Leaves me poor,

scorned again,

mired in want and envy,

as they run,

sick and tired

of my flapping frenzy.

<u>Testing Time</u>

It's testing time,

so fishing lines,

are dangling down,

on every side,

enticing me,

with baited flies,

to lure me on,

to my demise.

I dare myself,

to realise,

that they're all decoys,

in disguise.

Their mask belies,

what-ifs designed,

to trip me up,

and get a rise.

...

The slightest slip,

and it's implied,

that I'm inclined,

towards their lies,

but those are things,

I can't abide.

They leave my

frontal cortex fried,

as I rewind,

and itemise,

the sneaky slurs,

they slid inside.

Then one-by-one,

I neutralise,

till I can get on

with my life.

Unwinding with

some stifled sighs,

I leave the scene

of crime behind.

...

Next time there'll be

no compromise,

I'll spot the early

warning signs,

and do jiu-jitsu

with my mind,

to sweep

the saboteurs aside.

Adage

Battered luggage,

battle damaged,

kicked around

the cargo carriage.

One good runner,

heavy mileage.

Have a rummage

through the silage.

Maybe find some

scraps to salvage.

Courage wrought

from rotten cabbage.

Safe and savage,

crappy marriage,

best this mannish boy

could manage.

Single sandwich,

last man standing,

till I make the

vultures vanish.

The Me-etnam War

Such strange accumulations,
I picked up along the way.
Where life meets limitations,
ugly things come out to play.

There's monsters in my garden,
now I'm scared to go outside.
My arteries have hardened,
and my tongue is getting tied.

I never will surrender,
if I do I'll lose my soul,
attacker and defender,
in a war for self-control.

If this was a position,
I'd abandon it and run,
eroded by attrition,
undefeated but undone.

Fish Oil Salesmen

A mouse fell into the water,
but realised he could not swim.
So, sinking, he started to drown,
and appealed to all those around,
to intervene and rescue him,
from his looming aqua-slaughter.

Luckily a timely blowfish,
adept at handling such crises,
saw him flailing in the distance,
so made haste to give assistance,
first clarifying his prices,
then giving a diagnosis.

"Right", he uttered in bubbly tones,
"The thing is you think you're a mouse,
but here you need to be a fish,
or your life force will diminish.
So from now on try to arouse
those hidden fish-like chromosomes."

...

"I don't want to be difficult,

but isn't what you said bullshit,

designed to cover up the fact

you have nothing to counteract

this, but don't want to divulge it?

And isn't that unethical?

Not to mention unmedical?

The emperor's clothes aren't visible!

Would you put unreal bandages

on real severed appendages?

The idea's clearly risible!

But maybe I'm just cynical."

"Your bad attitude holds you back.

If you can't pretend you have gills,

then that only leaves one option:

I'll make you out a prescription

for some anti-mousation pills,

which ought to get you back on track.

...

Some side-effects that may arise:
mild extremity shrivelage,
aft bottomly gas explosion,
acute nippular corrosion,
loss of erectile privilege,
and an agonising demise."

"So it seems my choice lies between
pretending I'm something I'm not,
or strange pills that have the queerest
effect on all I hold dearest,
or just expiring on the spot
like a sailor on Halloween?"

And as his ordeal went on,
he saw other floundering mice
being treated by kindly blowfish,
with flashy degrees and trophies,
who charged them the ultimate price,
for the sea claimed every last one.

<u>Judas Switch</u>

Some bastard flicked my switch again,
the switch that tortures mortal minds,
by seeking out the fears in men,
and making doubts from what it finds.

It's time to cast my magic spells,
to straighten out the truths it bends,
to neutralise the lies it tells,
to fight it till the nightmare ends.

I'd like to meet the silly bitch,
who put this humbug in my head,
I'd thank him for his Judas switch,
then hide some spiders in his bed.

Horrid House

Your house has ice cream wafer walls,

a paper roof and balsa door,

there's eggshells scattered through your halls,

and trap doors hidden in the floor.

I'd like to come and visit more,

but when I do we end up hurt,

a walk-in one-man civil war,

where every word's a red alert.

I try to think of things to help,

but they don't help, they hurt instead,

I leave before you grab my scalp,

and try to cut it from my head.

I hope you go live somewhere new,

I hope we don't become estranged,

that horrid house just isn't you,

I think you're overdue a change.

Obvious Lies

All these obvious lies,

try to slip through the door,

dressed as truth in disguise,

sent to probe and explore.

Till my iron facade,

becomes battered and thin,

till they catch me off guard,

and they find a way in.

Then my job is to prove,

that a lie is a lie.

Though it doesn't behoove

me, I still have to try.

Not so much like a choice,

more a contract I signed,

to develop my voice,

until doubt is declined.

...

It's a difficult task,

I can't let any through,

and I'm too scared to ask,

what it means if I do.

So I stand at the gate,

watching thoughts that arise,

and I try to negate,

all the obvious lies.

Dark Horizons

These dark horizons hunting me,

I cannot catch my breath.

A creeping lack of certainty,

is choking me to death.

It doesn't matter what I try,

or how or where I run.

It shadows me and fills the sky,

to steal away my sun.

I try to fight, I try to hide,

I tap dance, I ignore.

Still every time I look outside,

it's darker than before.

Waking Demons

When I sleep I don't have nightmares any more,
but I have them when I wake or just before.
They're about the day the wolves break down the door,
and they tear my heart out on the bedroom floor.

In those moments it's as if my fears come true,
time to get a grip and do a quick review.
I return the thoughts I don't wish to renew,
books I didn't choose, now too long overdue.

Oh for mornings that unfold all lazy smooth,
mind and mattress intertwined deep in a groove,
less electric shock and more a cosy ooze,
waiting till I'm in the mood to make a move.

I have dreams in which I wake like that again.
Guess it's possible but I can't picture when,
with a mind marooned inside a lion's den.
I just want to wake the way I did aged ten.

<u>Serenity</u>

Sweet unreachable serenity,
show me your face,
for old times' sake.

Lift me up,
take me in your arms,
let me sleep in your lap.

Pluck the nails from my palms,
soothe the folds from my brow,
bathe me in your warmth.

Remind me what it is to know love,
until I'm mended enough,
to climb back down into the asylum,
and be broken once more.

<u>Shadow Shiva</u>

Who are you?
You dream spoiler,
spanner in my works,
crusher of new leaves,
innocence defiler,
the catch that always lurks,
prince of equanimity thieves.

The same old adversary,
I've been fighting all my life.
Happy anniversary,
my shotgun wedding wife.

I never used to see
your sneak attacks,
timed perfectly,
aligned back-to-back,
to sabotage me.

...

But I learned to weigh

the usual precursors,

gauge darkness holding sway,

smell milky wet nurses

waiting in the wings,

aching to suckle

the latest bastard spawn

your violation brings.

Satan's brood put to breast,

inside cuckolded dreams lying torn,

misappropriated precious things

fashioned into a nest,

to cradle our foul offspring,

whom I'm blackmailed to feed;

lest their demented cries,

sow my mind with Devil seed,

which never dies,

but breeds inside,

or damn my eyes,

I must commit infanticide.

...

Either way you win,

you murder sweet hope,

with demons born in sin,

birthed by succubus bitches,

like pubes placed in my new soap,

like unscratchable itches,

planted underneath my skin.

Sick sadistic shadow Shiva,

hunting me all my days,

misplaced misanthrope,

serial dream cleaver,

following me close always,

chasing me onto the end of a rope

and sneering as you pull the lever.

Hell Hole

I can't tell when I fell down this well,

but I'm stuck with the Devil in Hell.

I would crawl up the walls but alas,

they were cut from impassable glass.

He's so happy I'm trapped down this hole,

a chance windfall for him to control.

On a drip-feed of fear and despair,

he delights as I tear out my hair.

I refuse to abandon all hope,

so I use the old hair to make rope,

and old toe nails to fashion a hook.

I grow more in the time that it took.

One night soon when the Devil's asleep,

I'll climb up without making a peep.

Once I've finished that happy ascent,

I'll drive back with a truck of cement.

Alan E. Retentive

When a thing is left unfinished,
then my peace of mind's diminished.

If you don't put things away,
I'll turn into Reggie Kray.

Wading in without preparing,
leaves me sighing and despairing.

When I see a corner cut,
it's like scissors in my gut.

Not selecting the right tools,
leaves me sweating swimming pools.

If you don't pay full attention,
I will put you in detention.

Please don't give me bad instructions,
or it's going to end in ructions.

When a thing gets badly done,
I'll insist it's rebegun.   ...

I'm afraid I can't abide,

with loose ends you left untied.

If a plan is changed last minute,

then I'd rather not be in it.

If you change it half way through,

then no Christmas card for you.

<u>Hope</u>

You little fickle phantom hope,
in my back pocket yesterday.
You leapt out like a bar of soap,
slipped through my hands and flew away.

I need some wings that won't fly off,
when I grow tired or turn my head.
Gains won so hard are lost too soft,
you're like the wind it's often said.

The Me You're Meant to See

I have to dance alone a while,

so walk away and leave me be.

I doubt you'll dig my dancing style,

it's not the me you're meant to see.

Excuse me while I hit eject,

but this is an emergency.

I'm in a spin I can't correct,

it's not the me you're meant to see.

You have to let me disappear.

I can't though if you look at me,

cos while I'm gone, the one left here,

is not the me you're meant to see.

A Safe Place

How can you say with a straight face,

that I'm in a safe place,

that I can tell you anything?

When you're a complete stranger to me,

in an opportune arrangement,

with a private healthcare company,

mutually profiting from my misery,

milked in measured perpetuity.

No, you're in a safe place lady,

having play dates with the crazy,

then escaping to your dream home,

knitting booties for your baby,

wafting steam in treacle tones,

supposing that maybe I'm just digging holes,

when I'm slaying giants here to reach my goals.

So why dress it up like I'm carrying coals?

Why pull a face like I'm chasing my tail?

Why spin a hard-earned win into a fail?

...

Well I don't dig how your forked tongue rolls,

twisting my good news into a boomerang,

blindsiding me with a sly left hook,

a little later than the boxing ring bell rang.

Is this what your expert taught you in your textbook?

It's easy for you to say from your safe place,

with your three holidays a year,

and a winning place in the human race,

but I'm living in a loser's hell here,

and all you do is lean on me, to tell

you all my dirty little secrets,

cos it's vital to your process.

Don't you think I haven't noticed,

it's the same routine regardless,

with my secrets or without?

The same old cure you always tout:

to just ignore the nagging doubt.

OK, so how about I set your hair on fire,

but you can't get up from your chair to put it out?

                                                        ...

All too easy to say from your safe place,

with your new BMW parked

in your private parking space,

while I rummage around off-site,

fumbling through the damage in the dark,

searching for the right face,

to re-engage your revolving door,

with a faked air of grace,

and not the choked roar

of bitter rage I really feel.

A once-proud lion brought to heel,

pacing an ill-fitting cage,

yearning for a safe place.

<u>The Puzzle That Is Me</u>

I'm fed up with the puzzle that is me,

the crossword's like a gift compared to this.

I lack the wit to set the letters free,

entrapped in fractured words that went amiss.

I'm pig-sick of the puzzle that is me,

Sudoku seems so easy to me now.

My rows and columns don't seem to agree,

the numbers got away from me somehow.

I've had it with the puzzle that is me,

the Rubik's Cube's got nothing on this thing.

I can't match up these colours in 3D,

no matter how much blood and sweat I bring.

I'm finished with the puzzle that is me,

it's not so much a puzzle as a trap.

The trick is not to solve it but to see,

that sometimes fact and fiction overlap.

<u>Sticky Labels</u>

I used to be a loony.
Bein' a loony sure is lonely,
cos I thought I was the only one,
and bein' a loon, my friends had gone.
Your friends can't be depended on,
when you are not like them.

Now I'm a loony with a label.
Hey I'm mentally disabled!
Now it's OK bein' unstable,
cos there's books with graphs and tables,
but beware those who finagle,
all the lovely loony money.
Now the welfare think I'm idle,
and they treat me really funny.

...

Guess the label's lost its novelty.

The shrinks don't see the real me,

they see a live commodity.

It's all revolving doors you see.

They profit from my misery,

to get them cars and property,

while I'm stuck here in poverty.

It's daylight bloody robbery.

I think I'll ditch the label now.

It doesn't help me anyhow.

I'll be a loony like before,

no label, no revolving door,

no glib unhelpful narratives.

And pardon the pejoratives,

I'm pretty sure I've paid my dues,

just check the bottoms of my shoes.

I made an art of how to lose,

I don't just mean my mind.

Mandelbrot Upset

Whenever there's an error on the screen inside my brain,
I send two neural coders in to remedy the pain.
But sometimes they get errors in their brains the same as me.
The problem starts proliferating exponentially.

I thank them for their trouble and I send them for a rest,
but then I have to double back and spray the hornets' nest.
Unable to unravel all the threads back to the bug,
I call up my headquarters and I have them pull the plug.

The status goes to DEFCON 1, the lights all turn to red,
my bombers rain down atom bombs till everything is dead.
I rest a hundred years until the radiation's gone,
then once the debris's cleared away I try to carry on.

<u>F9</u>

Temporal leaks,

loss of control,

years pass like weeks,

down a black hole.

Must make it stop,

stop and restart,

start from the top,

this time with heart.

Supermarket OCD Avalanche

It was all going surprisingly well until the fruit and veg',

when a word I heard made time stand still,

and moved me to dredge,

for the mantra to prove that it's not what I fear,

so I can disarm this bomb and sound the all clear.

But somewhere deep in the unlit caverns of my mind,

I know that it won't be long until I'm inclined,

to find new bait,

to reel myself in, ever closer to that state,

where it feels like the weight of the world is on me,

where there's no escape from my mind's self-rape.

Nowhere to run and hide,

to decloak and save my pride,

from the nefarious traps it sets,

cos no matter how bad it gets,

I'm stuck inside this temple to Hermes.

...

I already tried return journeys,

but it doesn't work out so well.

You end up back in the exact same place,

minus petrol and time, with egg on your face,

but always without a towel.

"Spillage in aisle three!".

I'm sure that man and woman are following me,

we made eye contact back by the pork.

Wait, can they hear my mind talk?

Now back to that thing about the word,

where can I stand so I won't be disturbed,

or hectored or jostled or rudely observed?

Over here, there's a space by the lemon curd!

Nope, now it's the spot in the shop that's preferred.

Oh, how absurd!

No recipe I ever heard uses lemon curd.

...

I can't even hide by the cushions and bedding,

are these fuckers being sent here to do my damn head in?

It's as if they all KNOW, and they're working out when,

it's the pivotal time to play hell with my Zen.

If there was a mindfuck scale, this would be ten,

or it'd keep on past zero, and start at one again.

A new aisle, a new hope, a new chance to take a new run,

at the karma deficit I've accrued since the upset in aisle one.

But now three more jokers have dealt their way in,

my mind's fickle focus is frayed from replaying,

havoc, stuck thoughts run amok.

I'd forgotten how much supermarkets can suck.

Got to pick a spot and try to make a ruck,

so this ball of knotted mind wool I can finally unfuck.

Little improvement as I limp down aisle four,

a small dancing girl slips and falls down on the floor.

Inner-trigonometry, angling all the while,

performing an exploratory: "am I a paedophile?".

And it doesn't even matter that I know it isn't true,

the seed of doubt is planted, so it's crucial I pursue,

an epic legal defence at my sanity's expense,

so clarity's restored and doubt is shifted off the fence.   ...

But once that case has been thrown out,

new allegations will arise no doubt,

about grandma on checkout three,

really being my cup of tea,

even though she ain't,

or worse still it'll repaint

her face with the face of my sworn enemy.

AAAAAAAAAAAAARRRRRGGGGGHHHHH, triple threat!!!

Starting to smell my own sweat, so I bet they can too.

OH FUCK YOU!

This aggression shall not stand!

Enough of this slander right now, I demand,

a brand new jury of peers comes and hears,

one final defence to allay ALL these fears,

to bundle them up and put them to bed,

once and for all so I can unhook my head,

and get back in the moment, and shop like a PERSON.

...

... but now I've thought "bed" so the gears start reversing ...

my next legal defence I'm already rehearsing,

my Satanic luck cursing,

my brain pipes are bursting,

with unresolved threads,

of children and murder and bad words and beds.

And there's that man and woman who've been following me.

How the hell'd they get here so quick all the way from aisle three?

It makes no sense ...

unless they were sent ...

especially to persecute me?

And that elderly man, hanging round where I am,

over there by the rice, and now here by the jam.

You cannot be serious?

Mind aching, delirious,

down by the Cheerios.

                                                              ...

I'd like to put my hands around his neck,

and choke him out,

but I'm stuck up in the upper deck,

so all I've got's a rout.

So I scuttle away to the baking stuff,

pretending I'm intently studying puff-

pastry for some complex recipe,

of earnest necessity,

when all along I'm secretly trying to convince myself,

that the word on that mince-meat,

is separate to the bad idea in my head,

tangentially associated via a barely traceable thread,

to some trouble long ago,

of which no one can know.

...

That's why I juggle whatever it throws,

ducking or taking body blows,

while all the plasma flows,

up from my bloody nose,

to my brain,

to take up the strain,

of a mind baulking under the onslaught,

of insanely too much thought,

and simultaneous close-quarters jousting.

Dripping subcutaneous waters, dousing

me in my own fluid,

auto-baptism by a self-flagellating druid.

And by the time I start to get a handle on this thing,

recursively tying off all the loose bits of string,

the irony is it doesn't even really matter,

cos now all I can hear is the chitter and the chatter,

of chiming beer cans and clinking bottles,

as shell-shopped captives grip white knuckles,

round trolleys flying down the final aisle,

picking up a prize for their miracle mile.

...

But for this non-runner, it can only mean,

that there's just one thing left to get,

and that's a magazine.

Then it's off to the checkout,

where I'll stick my neck out,

to act like I'm normal,

with an over-informal nosy stranger,

going through my hoard,

opaquely judging my choices,

cos she's bored.

Wait, can she hear these voices?

Just go through the motions,

performing final devotions,

to the god of mass-produced processed crap,

praying there's no final lurking mishap,

like my card isn't recognised,

by the cyborg mechanised life-audit machine.

...

126

And no obscene thoughts,

about the chick in tight shorts,

two people behind in the queue.

Boy what I'd like to do ...

NO NOT TO THE CHILD NOR THE OLD MAN BEHIND HER!

And that gives me the usual painful reminder,

that I can forget about anything like that,

because I'm one seriously unwell cat,

with a lot of bad news under his hat.

So that folks ... is that.

Settle up with the woman,

and dig deep down to summon,

the missing gear required,

to drive home this tired

mental patient,

from his latest self-violation.

Kool-aid

Mother hens with calming voices,
smother you with mainstream choices.
Bare your soul and share your vices,
let them tear your life to pieces.

Shave your hair off, look like Kojak,
drink the Kool-aid, take the Prozac,
get a job and get a tie rack,
Kansas City shuffle hijack.

Don't make trouble, that's for losers,
negative bad vibe abusers.
Get your head right, get to Pfizer's,
join the flock and share the prizes.

When your gut screams doubts unspoken,
they'll insist your mind is broken.
Blind to truths they've long forsaken,
they're asleep, but you've awakened.

Food Fight

Sat around the table,

mincing words and munching meat.

Not sure if I'm able,

to act cheerful and discreet.

Scanning round their faces,

get a grip on the gestalt.

Try maintaining stasis,

when I'm asked to pass the salt.

Wish I could switch places,

just to witness how it felt,

to dwell inside the spaces,

where the bad ideas melt.

Trapped beneath the table,

civil war between your feet.

Wrestling to re-label,

and get back up on my seat.

<u>Snakes</u>

Felt stronger yesterday,
but the feeling slipped away.

It melted while I slept,
when I woke and saw, I wept.

Of all the ground I'd gained,
not a single piece remained.

New leaves are hard to turn,
when you've seen too many burn.

<u>Attrition</u>

I'm grappling with a demon in my mind,

he's crapping on whatever he can find.

He tries to make me lean,

towards the things that I don't mean,

until I'm forced to stop the music and rewind.

He lurks around the things I love or hate,

and works on cracks so doubt can infiltrate.

He throws in a grenade,

I have to ditch the plans I made,

and put the pin back in so it won't detonate.

Like Cato taking Clouseau by surprise,

a quick defence I have to improvise.

He devastates my flow,

while I devise a Judo throw,

to show him master-servant protocol applies.

It's hard to keep your sparkle as a slave,

your heart's engraved with scars each time you're brave.

The fighting makes you old,

the lighted embers fade to cold,

this stifled life will put me in an early grave.   ...

So tired of always being on red alert,

of salvaging my diamonds from the dirt.

One day this war will end,

and I can finally ascend,

to free the real me from all the blame and hurt.

Revolving Door

Psychologist earns,

prescription drugs cloak concerns,

revolving door turns.

<u>Waste</u>

Civil war inside my head bone,
neither side is backing down.
Decades wasted in the dead zone,
pacing trenches with a frown.

<u>Introvert</u>

I've always been an introvert,
your social contact makes me hurt.
Some days it's better, some days worse,
on those days, someone fetch a nurse.

In acts of social décollage,
I leave to let my soul recharge.
My friends think there's a thief at large,
they say I'm half-man, half-mirage.

The extroverts aren't filled with dread,
when into crowded rooms they're led.
Of extroverts it can be said:
they rush in where we fear to tread.

A burden that I can't ignore,
I've got a thorn stuck in my jaw.
Regarding using my front door,
I've learned for me that less is more.

...

One day I'll travel to the stars,

no more "how are you?"s and "ha ha"s,

a place without loud cocktail bars,

a one-way solo trip to Mars.

Nuts and Bolts

When my short-term memory fails,

I can't recall the small details.

Things you people take for granted,

go astray and get supplanted,

with gaping voids and question marks.

The signal goes but nothing sparks.

Where "sure" should be, an empty room,

a clog wedged in my neural loom.

So I go back and check the bolt,

to generate that extra volt,

to budge the gear that will not shift,

to give my wilted mind a lift.

Then I can put the doubt to bed,

and move on with an unclenched head.

But I won't make it very far,

before I'm staring at my car,

to watch the locks jerk up and down,

refining focus with a frown,

to try and capture what has flown,

repeat until I feel it's known,

that up means bad and down means good.   ...

I need to feel it's understood.

And clockwise means the gas is on,

is that a zero or a one?

Just ascertain it's on the line,

that's all they do and they seem fine.

Re-turn the key, re-slide the bolt,

scant solace that it's not your fault.

If something bad slips through the net,

I can't forgive and can't forget,

nor carry on nor comprehend.

Please God just make this madness end.

Ludovico Van Beatover

I like to sabotage myself six ways before breakfast,

tourniquets and turned-off taps mitigate the tempest.

Crashed up hard against my own cruel limitations,

learned early not to settle for superior imitations.

I habitually impale myself upon the truths I see,

more ordnance for marauders to carpet bomb me.

Wracked by wrong people who all believe they're right,

well let them have their day, because I own the night.

<u>Defiance</u>

Test old patterns,

learn from praxis,

flat refuse to pay your taxes.

See what happens,

tap dance past it,

navigate outside the abscess.

Panic flattens,

doubt collapses,

dead what-ifs and drowned perhapses.

Bad Day

Bad day,

bad forces hold sway.

Why's it always have to be this way?

Any time I scrape some time and space,

trick cigars blow up in my face.

Too tired of this stale routine,

of struggling up again,

and scrubbing myself clean,

of running to my pen,

and snuggling up with what I mean.

Wish I could cut away the rot,

tie a knot and chop if off,

then carry on with what I've got,

minus a madhouse full of stuff,

and a madman with a cough.

...

But I can't, so I persist,

try not to count the years I missed.

Too scared to open up my wrist,

I bludgeon on,

though hope has gone.

I do not live, I just exist.

<u>Superman</u>

Supernova,
seconds out,
loony rover
sent to scout,
looking over
ancient doubt.

Superstitious,
sticky thoughts,
slippy fishes
vainly fought,
look delicious
till they're caught.

Supersonic,
speed of sound,
flocks of phonic
spears inbound,
right mnemonic
puts them down.

...

Super soldier,

never quit,

don't indulge the

counterfeit,

dark nostalgia,

done with it.

Event Horizon Oblivion

Assured that your mission is under control,
you drift without knowing towards a black hole.

Too slow to pre-empt your precarious plight,
you can't quite persuade all your engines to light.

Harsh pressures and forces you've not before known,
contorting your vessel and making her moan.

The panic and dread leave your head in bad shape,
too addled to conjure a plan of escape.

Drawn headlong at light speed into the unknown,
ensnared, disbelieving, so scared and alone.

What's left when you've weighed up no options remain?
No struggle, no come back, no hope to regain.

Just shut down your systems, relax and sit back,
get ready to lose yourself into the black.

The Gift That Keeps on Giving

Head spilling over with what-ifs,

full plus a further thirteen fifths.

I'm badly wired and bloody tired,

of these surprise unwanted gifts.

You see I've seen it all before,

it's non-stop opposites galore.

I spot a doubt and bail it out,

but it's not long until there's more.

I built a dam to hold them back,

so I could get my life on track,

but bombers pounced with bombs that bounced,

and it got cracked in the attack.

So I just keep on keeping on,

I take the doubts on one-by-one.

Here at the grindstone in my mind,

I'll smooth the corners till I'm gone.

Maximum Whelm

How I dream of being just whelmed,

I can't remember how it feels,

I am drowning in a realm,

filled with impossible ordeals.

There's no resting place or crutch,

the torment follows me around,

trouble whelms me much too much,

and there's no solace to be found.

How I wish I was a child,

before the whelming reached its peak,

when the whelms were meek and mild,

and let me win at hide and seek.

<u>You're Welcome</u>

Returning from a vulgar pause,

I said my mind is not like yours.

It creeps up on me by surprise,

a wolf inside a lamb disguise.

The gifts it gives me to unwrap,

turn into vipers in my lap.

Held hostage with no place to hide,

where fear and bad ideas collide.

That thing that we discussed before,

just does not matter any more.

I shut the door and lock you out,

it's just for me, my dance with doubt.

I'd tell you if I thought I could,

come close to being understood,

but where I go is not for you,

you lack the lens to view it through.

...

Take solace when I drift away,
that I keep hidden hags at bay,
who'd seek to weave their wicked spell,
and send you unbeknownst to Hell.

So pull your face and do your worst,
reactions which are well-rehearsed.
Just know before you lay your blame,
that I slay demons in your name.

<u>The Fall</u>

It seems as though I've fallen down again,

I'm unaware I'm falling till I land,

such things are always dangers when your brain,

was built on top of ever-shifting sand.

I'll try and bend my body to the storm,

it seems to take less damage when I do,

wrapped up until the weather feels more warm,

locked in until the skies appear more blue.

For now my friend I must go on alone,

to hide out in my tumbledown retreat,

to dance the only dance I've ever known,

to find a way to get back on my feet.

<u>Firefight</u>

Sly sirens flirting with my thoughts,

they're flinging dirt in from the dark,

until my certainty distorts.

Sly sirens flirting with my thoughts,

fight fire with firemen of course,

they pour cold water on the spark.

Sly sirens flirting with my thoughts,

they're flinging dirt in from the dark.

Too Slow

Once again life grates against the grain,
grim augurs I'm not apt to entertain.

The future collapsed as I slept,
insidious forces crept up in the night,
too slow of wit to intercept and make it right.

The idiot sits in the runaway train,
wondering where the steering wheel is kept.

<u>Pure O</u>

Pure O,

puerile,

panic in the booze aisle.

Saddle up this burro,

and take it on a rodeo.

Bluto,

blighting

Popeye's life with fighting.

Only so much sumo-

wrestling sailors want to do though.

Cumulo-

nimbus,

shivering me timbers.

Loathed to hit a new low,

so we stagger back to Truro.

Biro,

broken,

so a spell is spoken.

Can't commence a new row,

till I purify the bureau.   ...

Pluto,

schizo,

dancing a calypso.

Ate a bad potato,

now he's turning into Cujo.

Judo,

jackal,

floors me with a cackle.

Counter with a new throw,

and denounce him in the dojo.

Mojo,

Midas,

meddling inside us.

Highs 'n lows in solo,

like a masturbating yo-yo.

Fluvo-

xamine,

serotonin famine.

Side effects accrue so

life is passing by in slow-mo.

...

Neuro-

trauma,

patch up the performer.

Science smacks of pseudo,

and their pills are a placebo.

Dodo,

detected,

whom has it infected?

Like a game of Cluedo,

better pray that it's not you though.

Man Against Mind

Man against mind,

the outcome's unkind.

Civil war drains,

what spark still remains.

Brain Malfunction

Treacherous thoughts wrack my brain,
consuming all my days.
The driver derails the train,
firemen start a blaze.

Devils calm in prayer,
cops commit a crime,
barbers add more hair,
poets refuse to rhyme.

Clowns breed displeasure,
Santa Clauses steal toys,
Pirates discard treasure,
Spocks befriend McCoys.

Lives taken by a midwife,
archaeologists break what they find,
well-intended reason runs rife,
Judas logic crucifies my mind.

Breach

No!

Panic

Intruder

Battle stations

It needs removing

No rest until it's gone

Everything on lockdown

Follow quarantine protocols

Target and neutralise the hunter

until the fox is out of the henhouse

The Onion Field

I'm running through the onion field,

my woes a liquid load to yield,

they make me weep when they get peeled.

I came to claim a simple high,

the pills I take won't let me cry,

that's creepy even for a guy.

They've stuck a spanner in the gears,

that turn the taps that makes the tears,

it sucks when science interferes.

So I came here to take them back,

I crammed sad pictures in my pack,

to browse and breathe until I crack.

<u>Filter</u>

This mind is under audit,
several thousand times a day.
Well, not that I record it,
but it feels like it's that way.

My thoughts work up a hunger,
for the things that cause me harm.
the rug's pulled clean from under,
inner-certainty and calm.

I have to run for cover,
and replay the moment through,
to quarantine and smother,
all the demons that accrue.

It doesn't even matter,
that I know it's all untrue.
Such allies tend to scatter,
once the enemy breaks through.

...

So tired of being a filter,

for these fictions which aren't mine,

but till I've died or built a

wall, I'll try to hold the line.

Something's Wrong Here

Why did my dad's head and heart go so wrong?

Why has my life become a Pink Floyd song?

Why such problems with everything I touch?

Why so little, when I've given so much?

All brick walls and no elevator doors,

all debt ceilings and no hardwood floors.

Is this some alternate universe,

where all is corrupted and perverse?

Where something's fundamentally wrong?

Where things get placed where they don't belong?

Where the apple tree is poisoned at the root?

Promised apples, but delivered rancid fruit.

Maybe there's a universe where everything's alright,

where things go as they should do and me and Dad don't fight,

where we're not wasting time with who was wrong and who was right,

where every interaction isn't born from blame or spite,

perhaps we're even out there sinking cold ones in the sunlight.

It's beautiful ... but hard to believe, try as I might.

...

Still, if it somehow turned out to be true,

and while eating shit here, a small part of me knew,

that every bad thing in this reality,

was in some way benefitting the other me,

then that might put a different spin,

on this vicious circle I'm trapped in.

That might lift my head out of the brown,

when the shit storms come raining down,

and it feels like I'm gonna drown.

Some small solace for the rodeo clown,

who's finally run out of moves,

and feels the sting of the bull's hooves.

Cos these days, I dunno how much more time,

I can confine these bad ideas in rhyme,

when my fear of pain and the unknown,

is in real danger of being outgrown,

by this urge to make the trip to the place,

where I can meet my maker face-to-face.

...

Then I'll beg the lord of all creation,

for a long-awaited explanation,

as to why I got this broken brain,

and why my father's criminally insane,

and how a life so replete with pain,

could either deity or universe sustain.

<u>Skewered</u>

Sometimes my mind and I collide,
we disagree all through the day,
it's like there's saboteurs inside,
and they lay landmines in my way.

I say it's right, they say it's wrong,
I say below, they say above,
I say it's short, they say it's long,
I say I hate, they say I love.

I have to argue with myself,
to re-establish what I mean,
employing subterfuge and stealth,
in hope my madness won't be seen.

I'm sick and tired of being caught out,
I can't relax and think my thoughts,
plagued by these picadors of doubt,
trapped in the bloodiest of sports.

Hope Burn

I'm living in a hell,

as far as I can tell,

but when you say,

your life's that way,

it doesn't go down well.

The spiral never ends,

on fire as it descends,

and in the fall,

I lost it all,

my freedom and my friends.

I put my stock in hope,

a crutch to help me cope,

but hope was spurned,

and deftly turned,

into a hangman's rope.

I look up to the sky,

and beg God for a why,

but God's not there,

or doesn't care,

there's always no reply.

Interlude

Forgive me if I'm hesitant to laugh,
I promise you I don't mean to be rude,
I have to sort the wheat out from the chaff,
a sudden uninvited interlude.

Believe me when I say I'd rather be,
engaged and in the moment just like you,
but that's not meant for somebody like me,
so I'm afraid that this will have to do.

You'll get my full attention in between,
I'll try my best to make up for my lapse,
an actor joining halfway through a scene,
I'll improvise and cover up the gaps.

If only you could grasp what this is like,
I'm fighting for my soul while you relax,
abducted and impaled upon a spike,
besieged by lies that creep in through the cracks.

Remote Control

Vicarious living,

in the shadows I lie hidden,

watching others while I'm sieving,

through the tit bits they are giving me.

Imagining how life might be,

if I could do the things you do,

if it was me instead of you.

The could've-beens are heavenly.

Fulfilment is forbidden, see.

I learned to read telemetry,

and step back from the precipice,

cos certain things are recipes,

for shining lights on missing parts.

I'm well-versed in the arcane arts,

of sticking to necessity,

and stopping short of red alerts,

cos when I'm caught my belly hurts,

and you'll see how my psyche works,

Well that's just not acceptable,

the rot is not correctable.

I'd rather leave some mystery,

perpetuate a myth of me,

that's better than reality.   ...

So I pre-empt potential traps,

the harbingers of mind collapse,

and strike those places from my maps.

I should have been a monk perhaps?

But in the meantime I'll sit tight,

I'll watch the others day and night,

and mimic moves inside my head,

till it's not them, it's me instead.

<u>Dear Ears</u>

It's not as mad as it appears,

this strange vendetta with my ears.

In fact I feel the same as you,

I wish my ears looked normal too.

But certain things I can't abide,

like imperfections left inside,

bits jutting out that don't belong,

to take no action just feels wrong.

There'll be no peace until they're gone,

dislodge them, then put Savlon on!

Conversely though, that makes things worse,

an avalanche I can't reverse.

The others start to get concerned,

they say my ears look badly burned.

I wish they wouldn't stare like that,

it's time to buy a Russian hat.

...

When you can't stand stuff out of place,

you'll spoil your ears to spite your face.

It's not the way I'd like to be.

Right, that's the last time, you will see!

Please Let Me Disappear Into the Ground

Please let me disappear into the ground,

so I don't have to feel this any more.

Erect a granite tablet on the mound,

inscribed with words which passers-by ignore.

Please let me disappear into the ground,

where I won't have to dread the next attack.

I'm tired of being abused and pushed around,

and feeling unequipped to fight them back.

Please let me disappear into the ground,

if nothing follows this then that's just fine.

I'm ready for oblivion unbound,

it's better than this horror show of mine.

Please let me disappear into the ground,

the world won't bat an eyelid when I'm gone.

The King of Pointless People I'll be crowned,

the bottom rung the others climbed up on.

...

When life grows dark, false hope is not your friend,

it's best to trust your instincts I have found.

I feel like I have reached my journey's end,

please let me disappear into the ground.

On the Brink

I'm standing on the brink.

Things get kind of tricky here,

treacherous and sticky here,

beasts and goblins interfere,

with what I meant to think.

A prisoner of doubt.

Try new ways to get away,

tell it you refuse to play,

violates you anyway,

with protests or without.

I just can't see the point.

Tell me why this universe,

casts a curse you can't reverse?

Don't tell me it could be worse!

I'm gonna torch this joint.

The Ones We Fear

The fabled ones,
the ones we fear,
sequestered in a darkened room,
unageing sons,
locked in a year,
locked in an unbefitting tomb.

We fear the will,
that broke the rule,
that took them to the other side,
that took the pill,
that kicked the stool,
that cradled them through suicide.

Hoovering the Hoarder's House

Start off with a clean sheet,

marshal your forces to meet,

the vexatious task ahead,

with equanimity instead,

with a callous can-do face,

at an expeditious pace.

This time it will be better,

I won't do it to the letter.

Snappy actions from the wrist,

behold the silk purse alchemist.

It seems the hoarder's on a break,

so this auspicious chance I take,

leaping forward into action,

lifting dust with skilful suction.

Like a matador I'm prancing,

through the bathroom door advancing.

Once more, into the breach I say!

Once more, into the vacuum fray!

Hey go ahead mat, make my day!

I hang it up and have my way,

and sing myself a song, "Hey hey,

we're the Monkees!" ...

Then I hit the rubbish junkie's

wall of pain ...

Let it rain ...

Let it rain ...

Let it rain ...

OCD ricocheting 'round my brain ...

Oh here we go a-fuckin-gain ...

Skirt around the random bits and pieces on the floor,

try to simplify but then my mind can't help explore,

all the nooks and crannies where fluff and stuff can hide,

picking up and cleaning underneath can't be denied.

Guess we're back exactly where we ended up last time,

good vibe's out the window and my mood's turned on a dime,

started off with lemonade but now I'm sucking lime,

time to go Godzilla on the hoarding scene of crime.   ...

Knuckle down and kick into the usual routine,

lifting, rearranging, changing gears to try and clean,

every scrap of carpet I can reach against the odds,

scared to touch the edges, where he keeps his odds and sods,

like shoe laces and tassels and a thousand lurking hassles,

I can't remove them all because I haven't got the muscles.

If I stray too close the vacuum chokes and makes a sound,

sounds like broken robots with bad throats are being drowned ...

EEEEEEEERRRRREEEGGGGKKKKRRRRR

EEEEEIIIIIIEEEEEE!

WEEREEEERRGGRREEEERKKRR

JURGHURGHURGHURGH!

What is with that whining? Have I vexed the Hoover gods?

Sending me a warning while they fetch their lightning rods?

Difficult deciding when to strike and when to cede,

where to draw the line betwixt the garden and the weed,

how to twist your body in bizarre gymnastic feats,

knowing when to pick up bits of plastic and receipts.

...

On I go from room to room and ply my private dance,
trying to eschew a suicidal second glance,
wondering if I should clean around that pair of pants,
wanting to go back in time and get a second chance.

Pausing while I Hoover the marauders from my brain,
goaded by the hoarder who takes pleasure in my pain,
wondering what I did wrong to land myself back here,
cursed to make silk purses from a bloated hoarder's ear.

<u>Free Fall</u>

The saddest man in England,
is perched beside a wren.

He's cursing that he's single,
and he's not like other men.

He's sick of sad old sing-alongs,
about the last time when...

The swingers clang a jingle,
as the clock approaches ten.

Some strangers point and mingle,
underneath him up Big Ben.

His guts begin to tingle,
as he learns to fly again.

<u>My Old Friend</u>

Well it's just you and me now my old friend,
the rest all slung their hooks and went away.
Ironic how the one left in the end,
is not a friend with whom I wish to play.

You showered me with kindness years ago,
in times when I was suffering and scared,
but little did that trusting youngster know,
you'd turn on me when I was unprepared.

You used my fears and secrets in your game,
you questioned me and tried to catch me out.
When I tripped up you tortured me with blame,
and built a cage around me with my doubt.

There's nothing left to take now but my life,
but if I'm not alive that means you're dead.
Perhaps then you should give me back that knife,
so I can cut your body from your head.

<u>Running On Empty</u>

I'm taking heavy fire,

from a thirteen-pronged attack.

I throw a flaming tyre,

they throw bunker busters back.

It doesn't seem to matter,

how I fight or what I bring.

Things re-arrange to scatter,

my resolve into the wind.

I sometimes start to wonder,

if I've roused an angry god,

who doesn't deal in thunder,

or a lethal lightning rod,

but lulls me into thinking,

there's a happy life for me,

while secretly he's sinking,

all the boats I put to sea.

...

I'm flying like a yo-yo,

twixt persistence and despair.

It suffocates my mojo,

till my engine's sucking air.

Well now my tanks are empty,

hardest mission ever flown.

If I don't make re-entry,

guess I'm walking home alone.

<u>The Anglers</u>

The anglers fish between my ears,
they bait their hooks with bad ideas.

They catch my thoughts and paint them black,
then throw the horrid black thoughts back.

Back down into my murky mind,
with claws that scratch and teeth that grind.

I have to catch them in my net,
before I falter or forget.

Before I let them get away,
or else they could be here to stay.

I can't have horrid thoughts like that,
left swimming round beneath my hat.

<u>Cabaret</u>

This competition has revealed,
a brutal truth that's hard to hear.
Some folks are just born better heeled,
they come equipped with better gear.
It's not an even playing field.

The poor must go to greater lengths,
to keep the ball out of the rough.
They learn to fight towards their strengths,
because their all was not enough.
They have to give it fifteen tenths.

Yet that is still no guarantee.
This game dictates that most must lose.
To crave success consistently,
will only guarantee the blues.
Just be the best that you can be.

Or better yet, refuse to play.
Invent a game that you can win.
You stand a better chance that way.
Transform the game show that you're in,
into a one man cabaret.

Spiders

There's spiders locked inside us,
sitting watching what the fly does,
salivating in their webs,
biding time for fresh colliders.

Then their little spider legs,
take them flying in like tigers,
sinking fangs into their necks,
slowly sucking dry their prizes.

Yet we seem to be inept,
to decipher their disguises.
Guess it's tricky to expect,
unexpectable surprises.

<u>Escape Trajectory</u>

Tangled free fall,

death spiral,

got to bust out,

got to glide away,

correct my attitude,

pull my nose up,

not so steep to stall,

but gradually,

carefully.

Not any old way,

not settling for the

deliciously outstretched hoof,

of the flying Devil,

circling,

salivating sulphur,

probing with pressure,

waiting for weakness,

selling saving souls,

but playing for keeps,

always promising the penthouse,

but delivering the lower level.

...

Not his way,

but my way,

a new way,

a pure way.

Spin a brand new dream,

from a putrid frightened nightmare,

win this tap dance for the team,

like a fighting Fred Astaire.

The RIGHT WAY!

or not at all.

Spike!!!

Hey hospital woman stop staring at me!
I'm having a difficult time, can't you see?

I just left a piece of my soul on the road,
that truck cut me up and I thought I'd explode.

Right now my anxiety's ramped through the roof,
look inside my head if you need further proof.

When things get like this it's so hard to relax,
my mind wanders off down these treacherous tracks.

Such slippery demons are tricky to spear,
and when I kill one, two brand new ones appear.

My mind throws me doubts like it's throwing me blades,
it's making me juggle too many grenades.

I have to dig in here and see this thing through,
cos otherwise terrible things could come true.

It might look to you like I'm acting uncouth,
but I'm catching hell here, that's God's honest truth.   ...

Forgive me if I don't look quite how you'd like,

but this is the face of an OCD spike.

Bubble Wrap

Surviving in escape delusion bubbles,

repackaging a world I cannot face,

recolouring its terrors and its troubles,

with visions from a tolerable place.

It works until the spoilers and the smashers,

come looking for balloons to burst for fun,

they giggle as they twiddle their moustaches,

and catapult my bubbles till they're done.

They leave me there without my old protection,

a stranger in a world he does not know,

unsure of what to do or what direction,

a man without a bubble ought to go.

I try to keep on going but I struggle,

a dancer who's forgotten all the moves,

then finally I find a brand new bubble,

and suddenly my state of mind improves.

<u>Missing Parts</u>

Salvation hinges on this thought,
I really need to think it right,
I'm not the towel-throwing sort,
I won't go down without a fight.

But then it slips right through my hands,
the meaning falls between the cracks,
my mind is built on shifting sands,
it's hard to find the bricks it lacks.

I wipe the slate and try again,
I must bring all my will to bear,
to re-evoke and re-explain,
the missing parts that were not there.

The repetition wears me out,
it leaves me spent and quite morose,
this private battle with my doubt,
will last forever I suppose.

<u>[Fear Rodeo Senryū]</u>

The fear rodeo:
good days, I get to ride it;
bad days, it rides me.

The Gauntlet

This is where it all hangs in the balance.

The flow assassins sneaked in while I wasn't looking.

Caught with my pants down,

out among the others,

worst place,

exposed.

Furtive Blanche Dubois,

relying on the blindness of strangers.

The music stopped but no chair,

cos no one told me we were playing.

Need my A game to bring this nightmare home.

Multitasking bedlam.

Need to be up in my head to deal with this new threat,

but need to be down in my body to deal with everything else.

So I diffract and do both, strangely, and at a quarter speed.

...

Trains of thought in perpetual flux,

born and dying simultaneously in the miasma,

but this little piggy tripped the alarm.

This one I must keep alive,

locked down in quarantine,

until it's been processed,

to a level of cosmic satisfaction,

that's completely beyond my control.

Fanning the flames of an ephemeral ember,

that's racing to die just to spite me.

Too much and it sprouts three new heads,

not enough and it's lost forever,

taking a piece of my soul with it down into the abyss.

Resistance fighter turned Vichy traitor in the blink of an eye.

So just enough to keep it alive then,

until I can get clear of these shills,

that the Devil keeps placing in the way.

Woman out of doorway, nine o'clock,

inexplicably trying to walk through me.

Car sprung back on its haunches, three o'clock,

wiggling its backside, ready to pounce.   ...

Whichever way I go, they go too.

Such is the etiquette of interloper tango.

Anything to derail the process,

to drive a wedge between me and my prey,

long enough for it to make a clean getaway into the fog.

Visceral sat nav,

constantly recalculating the route,

to dodge tricky deals,

to find the golden path,

through the chaos minefield,

affording me the time and space,

to address the jaguar,

that just exploded into the room,

circling ever closer,

eyes widening,

licking its lips.

Keep the precious spark alive until I find a clear patch,

to carry out emergency battlefield surgery,

no audience, no complications, no interruptions.

...

If I'm lucky, a clear run of two minutes is all I need,
to focus my remaining energy into a laser beam,
and nuke it,
expeditiously,
with the right meaning.
A clean kill.

Put my house back in order.
Pick up where I left off.
Aaaaaaahhhhhhh ...

But it's like they know!

Out of nowhere,
new players emerge to join the fray,
always seeking purchase on my space or focus.
Knowing glances, poker tells.
They're in on the joke,
but sworn to silence.

...

Cars suddenly pulling up,

pulling out,

pulling in,

human drama broadsides,

cackling capricious fishwives,

unpredictable gaggles of trouble.

A giant tag team of demonic dancers,

in choreographed concert.

It would be darkly beautiful,

if it weren't so treacherously hideous.

A pack of bloodhounds with one sole aim:

to harry, distract, obfuscate,

so that I cannot address that which needs addressing,

so that they get one more past me,

steal one more spark,

irretrievably alter the dynamic of the struggle for my soul,

incrementally in their favour.

And then it's gone...

Unacceptable horror!

...

Crushed under the terrible weight of an immovable burden,

scrambling around on all fours,

sifting through cinders in a burned out mind,

frantically trying to find the loose end,

that just got snatched away from me.

If I can't retrieve it,

I call the time of death,

and reluctantly perform a one-size-fits-all benediction,

a transparent mockery for the thought surgeon.

Like hurling a dictionary at a crossword clue,

in desperate hope against reason,

that the right answer will somehow osmose into place,

via some cloaked benevolent magic.

If I do find it again,

first comes that oozing relief-gasm.

But time is of the essence now,

so quickly back into the game room,

now resembling the aftermath of a death metal concert gone wrong.

...

Foul half-digested emissions sullying the canvas,

furiously fuzzy,

blocked up passageways,

less impetus than before,

everything in retrograde.

Only one thing to be done:

wipe all the pieces off the board,

call a void game,

go back and start all over again.

uuuuuuuuuurrrrrrrrrrrrggggggggghhhhhhhhhh ...

Right then ...

No more Mr. Nice Guy ...

Time to get creative,

aggressive,

take the bull by the horns,

leap on its back,

and slit its throat,

before it even realises what's happening.

                                                        ...

Always good to aim high,
sometimes it even works.

We could be here some time.

I've stopped caring about how it looks now,
or trying to salvage peace of mind.

I lost the day's initiative already.

At this point I'll just be happy to get out of here alive,
and crawl back home to double-over and bleed out,
a little less inclined to take the trolley with the dodgy wheel,
back out around the supermarket again.

<u>Change the Record</u>

Old pictures reilluminate,
I see them in a brand new light,
appreciating far too late,
the vastness of my oversight.

Though not a symptom of neglect,
but rather of paralysis,
how cruel the gift of retrospect,
such impotent analysis.

Dumb Waiter

I ordered lamb, you brought me pork,

I asked for soup, you sent me veal,

you took away my knife and fork,

and left me sucking lemon peel.

I think your chef was trained in Hell,

he hides these spiders on the plate,

to terrify the clientele,

and make us hyper-ventilate.

Your bistro sucks, your staff are rude,

I wish the courts would close you down,

I wouldn't come here for my food,

but you're the only joint in town.

Threadbare

These days I wonder how much more,
aggression I can stand,
what mischief has this life in store,
to dash the dreams I planned.

These labours I cannot complete,
carve gargoyles in my soul.
They line the ring roads I repeat,
and watch me carry coal.

These lies I'd like to leave behind,
too buttered to disprove,
replaying in a tortured mind,
to cut a deeper groove.

These broken bones won't be reset,
they keep me stuck in place.
I carry wounds I can't forget,
behind a threadbare face.

Please

Please spirit me away,

from all this misery and care.

I want to taste a day,

that's free from worry and despair.

Please magic me anew,

and make my mind and body clean.

Review what I've been through,

and keep the worst of what I've seen.

Please let me live again,

outside this shroud of fear and doubt.

I can't remember when,

or how it was to live without.

Please set my soul alight,

and let me have another chance.

This time I'll learn to fight,

and beat inclement circumstance.

...

Please let me feel alive,

we'll dance together in the flow.

Untethered I will thrive,

and light the places where I go.

That Old Magical Thinking

Do you ever get the notion,
that your actions can dictate,
seeming unrelated outcomes?
Intervention changing fate,
destroying lurking phantoms,
with surgical devotion.

If you don't avoid the cracks,
then you'll make your mother ill.
It means you're into stealing,
should the drink you're holding spill.
To think a righteous feeling,
slays a bad thought in its tracks.

No contest can be won,
without your lucky charm.
Unless you say a prayer,
your child will come to harm.
And every second stair,
must be stepped over or redone.

...

Constant bad ideas,

cascading through your head.

So very much depending,

on what's done or what is said.

Looks like it's never-ending,

this fandango with your fears.

That old magical thinking,

has you deep under its spell.

Your normal life got swapped,

for a superstitious hell.

You don't know when you dropped

the ball and started sinking.

Regardless of the blame,

you know you've had enough,

of lies that make you feel

like you're responsible for stuff.

Allow yourself to heal,

and flat refuse to play its game.

Written in Water

Awash with fear, I cup my ear,
to hear the roaring wave's advance.
When it will hit I've no idea,
it's like a game of time and chance.

I've tried to swim to land before,
to cheat the bore through will alone,
but any time I near the shore,
a storm gets up and back I'm blown.

Resigned that I won't make it now,
I turn and keep afloat and wait,
the cornered prey rehearsing how,
to let life go and meet his fate.

Amygdalian Abduction

I don't know exactly when this game started,

when from the safe path my children departed,

when I allowed myself time and again,

to be hypnotised and led by the brain,

through fog-smothered swamps to forsaken lands,

where soles skip scorched across searing sands,

where up becomes down and black becomes white,

where cackling accusers torment my night.

Locked up alone with no food and no water,

no right of appeal, no mercy, no quarter,

obliged to devise an ingenious plan,

to escape and petition the ferryman,

to row me back home to familiar shores,

perhaps to collapse in a merciful pause,

to hope against hope it might be the last time,

that I tango at gunpoint inside the sublime.

...

But increasingly these days I find,

in negotiations with my mind,

I'm thwarting doubt's fork-tongued attorney,

point-blank refusing to remake that journey,

ignoring those alluring sirens' cries,

eschewing the expiation of lies.

Lashed to my ship's mast, standing fast, unfazed,

while illusion is gradually erased.

<u>So</u>

So spent,

the bad man's stones no longer make a dent.

So used,

exploited, re-insulted and abused.

So wrecked,

bereft the basic gestures to connect.

So tired,

of lacking the prerequisites required.

So void,

of all the things the happy me enjoyed.

So sad,

that this could be the only life I had.

So done,

with running when they fire the starting gun.

So what,

I know I damn well gave it my best shot.

<u>Secret Society</u>

Oblivious diaspora,

worry whisperers,

desolate desperate,

unwittingly separate,

ugly ducklings

sick of suckling

doubts and fears,

unsticking gears,

ducking and diving,

barely surviving,

reluctant siblings

hooked on nibbling,

children of a lesser god,

the lying squad,

wandering blind,

fumbling to find

an answer

to mind cancer,

bound by shared flaws,

unplanned detours

stuck on see-saws,

cursing common ground,

averse to sudden sound,   ...

rehearsing what works,

reversing what lurks,

anxiety sorority,

a life of sorry quality,

fragile fraternity of seconds,

analytically fecund,

furtively hurting,

flagrantly flirting

with unending uncertainty

behind a lace curtain,

doubtful double agents

containing the contagion,

Manchurian candidates,

security demanded it,

Mercurial with tangly bits,

amygdalan army

holding back a tsunami,

stubborn Cnuts,

typos are a hoot.

Gone to Earth!

Gone to earth!
This restless night,
has left me quite,
bereft of mirth.

Gone to earth!
Compassion's thin,
on fashion's whim,
it's in a dearth.

Gone to earth!
An oubliette,
to resurrect,
a wrecked self-worth.

Gone to earth!
Beware the hound,
I'm safe and sound,
beneath the turf.

...

Gone to earth!

In my cocoon,

I lick my wounds,

and yearn rebirth.

<u>Möbius Trip</u>

The nightmare ends and spits you out,
but one foot's trapped behind the door.
It's snagged on strands of nagging doubt,
left frayed and unaccounted for.

Not fit to venture back that way,
you're forced to do a quick triage.
With towels or a tourniquet,
you fix the small and numb the large.

You try to fly toward the sun,
but vultures in the sky portend,
that something bad has rebegun.
The nightmare didn't really end.

<u>Reverse Engineering Mega-Doubt</u>

Waiting till I'm out of sight,

taking giant breaths repeatedly,

till my lungs feel like they're going to come unstitched,

till I'm giddy with oxygen,

till I feel like I'm gonna pass out,

till it feels... RIGHT.

Wondering if this deep breath deal,

is gonna give me a stroke,

or a haemorrhage one day,

but it's all I've got right now.

Turning the screws on my brain,

to squeeze out the bad feelings,

and leave just enough clarity,

so I can carry on about my work.

Cos I'm getting behind.

...

If only they knew that I'm doing two jobs here:

the one they know about,

and the one they can't know about.

The one I have to do on the down-low,

somewhere in the murky back alleys of my mind.

Working twenty-four seven for the resistance movement,

spinning plates to stave off impending doom.

Jolting my head forward violently to defy a bad idea,

making noises to ram the point home,

with the RIGHT meaning.

Straining every muscle in my head,

beyond the limits recommended in the owner's manual,

to manifest an intense grotesque grin,

that squeezes my brain so damn tight in the fist of my skull,

that it crushes into submission,

all the residual doubts and bad ideas.

Just so I've got enough space to move forward and do the next thing,

without being tripped up by razor wire every two steps.

...

But I know, whatever I do,

I'll be back here soon enough,

throwing familiar shapes,

dancing to this devil music,

that only I seem to be hearing.

Cute receptionist catches me,

doing extreme grin by the back door of the kitchen.

Wait - she's not even supposed to be here?

I planned it out and everything.

Now she knows.

She'll never look at me the same way now.

Damn, I really liked this one too.

Another one bites the dust.

Ironic hiatus,

as everything retreats to the tree line,

in solemn respect.

Like an enemy ceasing fire,

to allow the stretcher bearers,

to come out and collect the dead.

...

Fuck your pity,

you can keep it.

Just One More Fix

So powerful, like mind control,
this gift I have to fix it all.
I launch my thoughts like cannon balls,
to pulverise the fortress walls.

It clicks but it won't stick at all,
the bubble pops and back I fall,
it all resets just like before,
but now it's harder to recall
the mantra through the fog of war.

Around and round the depths I trawl,
around and round elliptical.

Unpowerful, ephemeral,
false feeling I can fix it all.
I guess it's what the doctors call
delusional or magical.

Bigger Fish to Fry

I've got no wife or family,

and they always wonder why.

Well pardon me but can't you see,

that I've bigger fish to fry.

They ask why I don't go outside,

and I answer with a sigh:

"Outside is where my tongue gets tied,

and I've bigger fish to fry".

Disowned because I don't watch sports,

"That's not normal for a guy!".

I just don't dig grown men in shorts,

and I've bigger fish to fry.

Been years without a woman's touch,

guess I'm too messed up to try.

I haven't given up as such,

but I've bigger fish to fry.

...

I live a life of solitude,

but it's not because I'm shy.

I hide because my brain is screwed,

and I've bigger fish to fry.

Itchy Scratchy Junkie

Hooked on scratching itches,

picking stitches,

checking messages,

secreting little packages,

as bait for praise and accolades.

Recharge these leaky batteries,

too quickly it evaporates.

Repeat six times till Saturday,

to make the feeling saturate.

Rotating gives me stomach ache,

a life replete with spinning plates.

I'm realising far too late,

the answer is to back away,

and let the blood coagulate,

shun itches like an apostate.

Can't find the off switch anyway.

Hope Alchemy

New day!
New lump of clay,
new chance to model it my way.

New day.
New dues to pay,
new consequences to delay.

New day!
New deck to play,
new queens and aces join the fray.

New day.
New brain decay,
new bad ideas to disobey.

New day!
New castaway,
new flotsam washed up in the spray.

New day.
New doubts to slay,
new ways to keep the wolves at bay.

...

New day!

New eggs to lay,

new babies hatching in the hay.

New day.

New disarray,

new strength to struggle come what may.

New day!

New things to say,

new words and pictures on display.

New day.

New thoughts astray,

new mind gymnastics and ballet.

New day!

New hope holds sway,

new feeling life might be OK.

Taking Out the Trash

Downward spiral, helter-skelter,

triggered when the Devil dealt a

sneaky blow below the belt,

the sharpest pain I ever felt.

It leaves a stain that's hard to clean,

it leaves me chained halfway between,

the waking world outside my head,

and inside chasing trails of bread.

It's time to gain the upper hand,

to separate the thoughts I planned,

from those the Devil shoehorned in.

I'll dump those in the rubbish bin.

<u>Unlike</u>

I make them cringe,
they brace themselves like taking a syringe,
they hold the back door swinging on the hinge.
I mustn't whinge.

They find me odd,
like I was tainted by the hand of God,
they skirt around the places where I trod.
The creepy sod!

It's a disease,
I seem to put the others ill-at-ease,
won't someone tell me how to fix this please?
Don't be a tease.

I guess I'm weird,
they send me in to get the riots cleared,
and one-by-one my friends all disappeared.
Could be the beard?

<u>Tired</u>

Tired of struggling forward through a lightning storm of lies,
tired of rounding corners walking into a surprise.

Tired of wearing shackles watching life pass by the bars,
tired of sneering jackals tearing open ancient scars.

Tired of scrounging courage to cajole myself outside,
tired of tripping up too soon and crawling back to hide.

Tired of being so tired of being so tired of being so tired,
life's so bloody tiring when your brain's so badly wired.

Suck-Ass Theatre

I'm in a three act drama,

I can see that clearly now.

I don't feel any calmer,

with that knowledge though somehow.

Act one is when you enter,

and the audience applauds.

You take the stage's centre,

and they bathe you in awards.

They tell you that you're special,

and that life is clean and fair.

You get a brand new satchel,

and a uniform to wear.

The second act is scary,

when the villains take the stage.

They make you sad and wary,

and they fill your heart with rage.

...

You meet your limitations,

when you try to fight them back.

Your foolish imitations,

shine a light on what you lack.

The third act holds a mirror,

and it offers you a choice,

to live your life in terror,

or befriend your inner voice.

To dwell inside your damage,

till it's all you really feel,

or ditch that toxic baggage,

and allow yourself to heal.

Well my play's a disaster,

guess it should've been rehearsed.

These lines I cannot master,

and I think the theatre's cursed.

<u>My Stupid Box</u>

My secret box,

which excess trauma and anxiety unlocks,

at first it helped me take the edge off all the knocks,

my box was tops.

My magic box,

it cast a spell to help me mop the tricky spots,

but then I couldn't stop the multiplying mops,

Pandora's box.

My crafty box,

it gave me thread to darn the holes in all my socks,

but then it tangled up the threads in horrid knots,

the two-faced fox.

My angry box,

I fed it ripples but it fed back aftershocks,

it shook my house apart and smashed up all my crocks,

best call the cops.

...

My Judas box,

it spun ad nauseam from innocent ad hocs,

I toss in pebbles and it spits out giant rocks,

it never stops.

<u>Shift</u>

A subtle change is in the air,

it came this morning on the wind,

a hidden shift, a latent tear,

a dark decree I can't rescind.

Its grim intent is understood,

it stripped the trees of all the birds.

I'd countermand it if I could,

alas I lack the magic words.

Behold those cold converging sounds,

the thud of hooves like rolling drums,

the huntsman's horn, the baying hounds,

for something savage this way comes.

Did I Ever Tell You How I Got These Scars?

I dream of being a UFO abductee,

in a flying medical facility,

where an ET with a medical degree,

performs futuristic surgery on me,

then beams me back to bed minus OCD.

<u>Sisyphus</u>

A gear keeps on sticking
in the front right of my brain,
it always leaves me tripping
on familiar terrain.

A gear keeps on sticking
in the front right of my brain,
some switches just aren't clicking,
so my certainty lies slain.

A gear keeps on sticking
in the front right of my brain,
I fear my head is splitting
from this frontal cortex pain.

A gear keeps on sticking
in the front right of my brain,
it lures me into licking
wounds that open up again.

...

A gear keeps on sticking
in the front right of my brain,
a chisel keeps on chipping,
but it goes against the grain.

A gear keeps on sticking
in the front right of my brain,
revisiting the missing
things I need to ascertain.

A gear keeps on sticking
in the front right of my brain,
it's hard to catch the chicken,
when you're in a ball and chain.

A gear keeps on sticking
in the front right of my brain,
repair the wound that's dripping,
and mop up the bloody stain.

A gear keeps on sticking
in the front right of my brain,
the spillage isn't wicking,
but just why, I can't explain.   ...

A gear keeps on sticking

in the front right of my brain,

it goads me into picking

over things that cause me pain.

A gear keeps on sticking

in the front right of my brain,

my donkey won't stop kicking,

as I ride it down the lane.

A gear keeps on sticking

in the front right of my brain,

fallacious doubts are tricking

me to fly into the flame.

A gear keeps on sticking

in the front right of my brain,

it tries to slyly slip in

things I cannot entertain.

A gear keeps on sticking

in the front right of my brain,

once more the scales are tipping,

bye bye sunshine, hello rain.   ...

A gear keeps on sticking
in the front right of my brain,
the needle keeps on skipping
to the start of the refrain.

A gear keeps on sticking
in the front right of my brain,
how quick the clock is ticking,
as my life goes down the drain.

Magic Mind

Raw, erratic, unrefined,
aspects of a magic mind,
not designed for what they need,
flapping round the things we find.

Don't tell us to multi-task,
made-up bunkum bankers ask,
nonsense born of wanton greed,
balderdash beyond our grasp.

Punish pegs for having souls,
hammer square ones into holes,
blame us when we start to bleed,
less like people, more like poles.

Levied, punished, pushed outside,
locked out by the ones who lied,
rocked the boat at ramming speed,
kicked out of a moving ride.

...

What to do when we don't fit,

life alone is dimly lit,

spinning flowers out of weed,

mind magicians never quit.

Long Live the Fighters!

This one goes out to all my brothers and my sisters,
bleached battle-hardened hands, caked in cracks and blisters.

Boxing our own shadows, disproving our own lies,
answering the *jumps* with our Pavlovian *how highs*.

Amnesiac checkers and monumental listers,
driving to distraction our Misses and our Misters.

Chasing that "right feeling" with the power to neutralise,
guardians against contamination's compromise.

Pure O fighters re-imagining tongue-twisters,
on the Western frontal cortex, we're like mental Sandinistas.

<u>I-con</u>

I talk about a god,
or devil in control.
With pitchfork and with rod,
they battle for my soul.

But those are just ideas,
I don't think they are real.
The metaphor appears,
to mirror how I feel.

My guess is they were tools,
deliberately made,
to make us follow rules,
by keeping us afraid.

So if along the way,
you spot those words entwined,
I think it's safe to say,
they're ciphers for my mind.

<u>Flirt Locker</u>

Sweet lady in the park,

I caught you looking back at me.

I haven't felt that spark,

since maybe 1983.

You glimpsed me through the fog,

off guard and chuckling like a child,

led headlong through the bog,

dragged by a dog rampaging wild.

I wondered what you thought,

and how you pencilled in my gaps.

I wondered if I ought,

to come and say hello perhaps.

But then it crossed my mind,

that I can't be that man for long.

I leave him far behind,

around the time my brain goes wrong.

...

You'd wonder where he went,

and I would make you ill-at-ease.

I wish they would invent,

a sodding cure for this disease.

Sweet lady in the park,

oh how it aches to walk away.

It's getting kind of dark

though, and I cannot talk today.

Window Shopping

Life abandoned in retreat,
staring from a back row seat,
watch them all devour the meat,
scraps rechewed don't taste so sweet.

Overlaps are rare and thin,
too much contact burns my skin,
gives a little window in,
envy's such an empty sin.

Caged emotion stirred and freed,
try to quash unanswered need,
turn it in and let it bleed,
ignorance is bliss indeed.

Poor Trade

I heave around a debt of care,

about those precious moments missed,

those times when I could not be there,

those doubts which I could not resist.

It's wrong of me to take the blame,

the missing wasn't mine to choose,

unbidden my accusers came,

with charges I could not refuse.

The parties, birthdays, Christmas days,

a love's first kiss and last goodbye,

all lost behind an absent gaze,

off fighting dragons on the fly.

How wicked it should come to pass,

that when it's time to taste the wine,

I'm trapped behind a wall of glass,

denied the gifts that should be mine.

Empty Lament

I take myself off in an empty lament,
a solace I sing through the unanswered pain,
the words may be tired but they're sung with intent,
there's no one to hear so my song is in vain.

I sing for lost youth and for love unfulfilled,
I sing for the sweetness I held but let go,
I sing for the castles my hands couldn't build,
I sing for the peace that my mind couldn't know.

My song is a thread through the story of me,
I splice a new length when there's pain in my heart,
it helps me recall how it all came to be,
a bundle of yarn I trace back to the start.

When hearts once so gullible harden and break,
when lacklustre lullabies don't hit their mark,
you sing your lament for your sanity's sake,
a map to help find your way out of the dark.

Fibby Pudding

As autumn wanes and winter looms,
the British finish off a dish.
In kitchens or in dining rooms,
with wooden spoons we make a wish.

You stir the mixture round and round,
towards yourself three times they say,
then make a wish but make no sound,
or else your wish gets washed away.

But when the bowl gets passed to me,
I pray my wish won't go astray.
My mind can twist a thought you see,
and wishes might come true some day.

I have to strain to clear my head,
to keep the tainted wishes out,
like those that wish for bad instead,
and those the Devil swaps about.

...

The hardest game I've ever known,

I have to really concentrate,

so when my wish gets set in stone,

no bogus wishes infiltrate.

Yet once a year I face my fear,

and stir the spoon and stand my ground,

and aim to make my wish sincere,

without a hiccup or a sound.

No Dibbity

Those born as dibs in a world built for dobs,

will find that they struggle to carry out jobs.

They cater for dabs, and even for dubs,

but dibs just don't fit through the doors of those clubs.

The best you can do is act like a dob,

work hard on your dobbing and run with that mob.

If that's too hard, be a dub or a dab,

they'll help you with anti-dib pills from a lab.

Don't buy their fibs about helping the dibs,

they're dirty damp squibs from political nibs.

They only care about voters on hooks,

who like how their insincere dib-concern looks.

And watch out for dobs who act like they care,

they'll put you on hobs and they'll simmer you there.

Take heed from a dib who's been round the block,

be more like the dobs or you're in for a shock.

Lost

My mind is setting tests again,
it's probing what I mean.
It's turned the surface of my brain,
into a trampoline.

My thoughts bounce back in poison ways,
and have to be rethunk.
I'm sifting through the ricochets,
and weeding out the junk.

If only I got paid for this,
to mitigate the cost.
I don't though, and it takes the piss,
just how much life I've lost.

A Beautiful Mind

We think that human beings should be standard,

our profit-hungry expectations pandered.

No physical disparities,

nor mind peculiarities,

but nature doesn't work so even-handed.

Instead it works by throwing out mutations,

by default, testing out the permutations.

A self-correcting system,

concealed intrinsic wisdom,

a slow computer churning calculations.

What right have we to question our beginning,

the force that set the stars and planets spinning?

Deliberate intention,

a cosmos of invention,

a Petri dish where life unbound is brimming.

Yet since we chose to leave our hearts behind,

in worship of the problem-solving mind,

we say nature got it wrong,

that certain aspects don't belong,

and we project a new design upon mankind.   ...

And God forbid you fall outside constraints,

this world no longer caters for complaints.

Then you'll be ostracised,

and obliquely penalised,

our pace dictates we quarantine the taints.

While we get tangled in this web of lies,

unwitting engineers of our demise.

creation carries on detached,

brand new anomalies are hatched,

and sometimes flies are really spiders in disguise.

Like someone who sees people that aren't there,

who starts up conversations with thin air,

who must be isolated,

locked away and medicated,

whose exquisite theory echoes everywhere.

Perhaps these fancy glasses made us blind?

A prescription far too eagerly defined?

Maybe the flaws we see as surplus,

were in fact put here on purpose,

and we ought to be in awe of such a mind.

Patterndaele

My troops are getting tangled in the wire,
the shells would brush it all aside they said,
but now they're in the open taking fire,
a civil war is raging in my head.

The trenches are encumbered with dead bodies,
they didn't stand a chance against the tanks,
moral has hit a low among the squaddies,
a mutiny is rumoured in the ranks.

My lads have battled hard and battled fierce,
but nobody can battle poison gas,
thank God our friends and families can't see us,
bent bleeding from the mouth in the morass.

It's costly fighting struggles of attrition,
you give it all you've got but it takes more,
I think I'll die defending this position,
what sin to waste a life on waging war.

Purge Overkill

Pray witness my confession,

I have things that I must share.

You give me the impression,

that you're capable of care.

There's monsters in my closet,

but it seems to be full up.

I left my last deposit,

in a Starbucks coffee cup.

Come listen to my horrors,

let me show you what I'm like.

I'll give you twenty dollars,

for some ribbons for your bike.

I'll tell you all the horrid

things I did that don't sit right.

They corrugate my forehead,

and they keep me up at night.

...

They don't match my idea,
of the man I'd like to be.
Relieve me of my fear,
help reveal the real me.

But if my stories bore you,
put my book back on the shelf.
In truth, they were not for you,
I was talking to myself.

Appendices

Appendix 1 - About OCD

Many of the poems in this book are about Obsessive Compulsive Disorder(OCD). OCD is an esoteric psychological phenomenon which was only identified relatively recently. As such, a lot of confusion still surrounds it, and it's often the subject of misconceptions. So I'd be remiss if I didn't briefly explain what OCD is for the uninitiated.

Once again though, I feel obliged to remind the reader that I'm not qualified in medicine, psychotherapy or pharmacology. This is simply a layman's understanding of OCD intended as background information for the poems in this book, and nothing more. If you would like a proper definition of OCD, then I'd advise you to seek out a recommended book on the subject written by an expert in the field. One that I've read which I'd recommend is Brain Lock by Dr. Jeffrey M. Schwartz.

I don't know what the preferred nomenclature is in medical circles, but for the purposes of this book I'll refer to somebody who has OCD as *an OCD sufferer*. It's just a label and no negative connotations are intended by its usage.

OCD is an anxiety disorder affecting the human mind. Sufferers are prone to developing *obsessions* which they subsequently devise *compulsions* to counteract.

Obsessions are tantamount to phobias which sufferers fixate on until the threat gets distorted to look increasingly worse than it really is. Obsessions can cover just about anything, but some common ones are: contamination, health, harm, sexuality, morality, infidelity, appearance, symmetry, and superstition surrounding words and numbers. Obsessions are in constant flux, and sufferers are likely to have several active at any given time. For each obsession, there will be a set of *triggers*.

Triggers are things that come up in everyday life, which an OCD sufferer associates with their obsessions in a negative way. A trigger could be a word, an object, a number, a song, a product, a substance, a person, a situation, a taboo, a perceived threat, or an *intrusive thought*. Just about anything really, but crucially, something that introduces unacceptable feelings of doubt into the mind of the sufferer regarding an obsession.

Like activating a tripwire attached to a root fear, the trigger leaves the sufferer with the overwhelming feeling that their fear might be true after all, or that some imminent threat is precariously looming. In the absence of a direct trigger, whatever the sufferer happens to be doing or thinking about is probed mercilessly for something to twist into a trigger. Indirect associations, opposites, double meanings, doctored memories. Something innocent transformed into doubt for doubt's sake. When OCD gets bad enough, the fear of being triggered itself will manufacture triggers out of thin air when nothing else is available. A bit like telling someone "Whatever you do, DO NOT think of a pink elephant!", and they immediately think of a pink elephant.

When a trigger occurs, the sufferer is suddenly catapulted into a state of high anxiety which, at its worst, is completely paralysing and utterly intolerable. It is incredibly difficult to ignore, and doing so feels like a violation of something sacred; a dereliction of one's solemn duty; like you're agreeing that it's OK for your worst fears to become true. It feels like you are deliberately choosing to give into dark forces if you don't take immediate action to counteract the threat.

Triggers are sometimes referred to as *spikes*, although the word can also be used in a larger sense to signify a general relapse in somebody's OCD.

Intrusive thoughts are sudden unwanted images or ideas that pop into the mind of an OCD sufferer out of nowhere, to act as a trigger. As with all OCD doubts, they are about things diametrically opposite to the sufferer's true values and preferences. There's a school of thought that everybody gets these thoughts to an extent, but while most people can easily dismiss them, people with OCD get stuck on them until they become triggers.

Intrusive thoughts can cover just about any kind of fear or doubt, but here are some common types:

- harm: about imminently hurting someone else or yourself.

- scrupulosity: about violating religious, moral, or ethical laws. These tend to affect people with religious beliefs, but they're certainly not confined to that. They can also be ideas that contravene one's own secular moral code.

- sexuality: about things outside your normal sphere of sexual preferences. e.g. straight people questioning whether they're gay and vice versa, or questioning whether you're into all manner of deviant things that you're not really into - incest, bestiality, paedophilia, necrophilia. Whatever you find most disturbing.

In my opinion, sexual doubts are the hardest aspect of OCD to explain to non-sufferers. I've even witnessed people with OCD getting the wrong end of the stick when fellow sufferers talk about this. Anyone with an understanding of OCD *should* know that these doubts are automatically false, just like every other OCD doubt. But when it comes to sexuality, people tend to have an atavistic sense of suspicion, especially when it comes to a feared societal bête noir like paedophilia. As a result, merely mentioning the word can arouse suspicion. For instance, imagine a married man with OCD trying to explain to his wife that the reason he froze up in the car just now, was that he had a sudden doubt about whether he was attracted to their son. She is going to need an awful lot of empathy and blind trust to accept that it's just a harmless symptom of OCD. More likely, she's probably going to be left wondering if there can really be smoke without fire, and whether OCD is just a cover story. It's hard to blame her under the circumstances. I really pity OCD sufferers who have the courage to be up front about these kinds of doubts, only for people to get the wrong end of the stick and condemn them. Everyone's a loser in that situation.

Compulsions are rituals that the sufferer intuitively devises over time to counteract these unbearable triggers. When a trigger occurs, the sufferer must perform the compulsion that corresponds to that trigger. They can't just perform any old compulsion in a slapdash, cavalier fashion. Oh no - it has to be the right compulsion, performed the right way, with the right feeling, without any mistakes or lapses in intention. On bad days, this can be infuriatingly difficult to accomplish, and that's why compulsions tend to involve some degree of repetition.

Some common compulsions are: checking, cleaning, re-arranging, confessing, reciting mental mantras, seeking re-assurance, and various body-focused repetitive behaviours like dermatillomania(skin picking), dermatophagia(skin biting/eating), and trichotillomania(hair plucking).

Once the compulsion has been carried out to the sufferer's exacting standards, the incident draws to a close and they're free to carry on with their day. OCD sufferers often refer to this moment as "when it feels right". This is when the panic alarm in your head deactivates, and you feel yourself passing over the brow of the anxiety hill, and back down the other side again. You gradually relax back into your normal state of mind, usually feeling mentally exhausted but relieved at the same time. For me, it's as if two giant fists unclench from around my brain and my gut.

Many sufferers report headaches and gut pains when their OCD is most active. It's widely known that anxiety affects the gut area so that one speaks for itself. Furthermore, it's been observed that OCD induces hyperactivity in certain areas of the brain, including the frontal cortex. So that probably explains the headaches. Some of my poems refer to these gut pains(*see A Tidal Mind and The Gauntlet*) and headaches(*see Testing Time and Sisyphus*).

Compulsions are the accidental offspring of a human foible called *magical thinking*. It's the same irrational belief system that convinces people they'll be struck by lightning if they walk on the cracks in the pavement, or that their football team will win if they put their right shoe on before their left shoe, or that walking underneath a ladder will bring them bad luck. Pragmatically speaking, those actions have no influence whatsoever on those outcomes. Yet for some reason we humans are terribly prone to buying into these artificial belief systems. Perhaps it's a placebo mind trick we unwittingly developed to self-hypnotise ourselves into thinking we have control over the uncontrollable.

I'll bet that everyone reading this has fallen under the spell of magical thinking at some point in their lives; no matter how innocuous it may have seemed; no matter whether you acknowledged it or not. Perhaps something as innocent as avoiding an unlucky number, or taking down your Christmas decorations on Twelfth Night, or wearing a lucky item of clothing for a job interview, or throwing a coin into a wishing well and making a wish. Perhaps even avoiding something completely harmless, because it's forever associated in your mind with something else that you fear.

For most people, magical thinking results in nothing more than delightful quirks or quaint superstitions. For OCD sufferers however, it's like pouring kerosene over a naked flame. It's the driving force behind their condition, because it makes them truly believe that their compulsions have the power to neutralise perceived threats. Think of a deluded fireman throwing paintings of the sea onto a fire, convinced that he's putting out the flames. Even in cases where the compulsion is somehow relevant to the threat(e.g. cleaning to counter contamination), it's highly likely that the perceived threat has gradually become so exaggerated in the mind of the sufferer, that the countermeasure isn't even necessary in the first place.

In reality, all that carrying out a compulsion does, is trick the sufferer's brain into deactivating the unbearable anxiety, so that they can return to their normal state of mind and get on with their life. Which sounds like a pretty neat trick doesn't it? But this brings us to the most unfortunate aspect of OCD ...

Compulsions have a cruel counter-intuitive quality to them. From the sufferer's point of view, it feels like they can stave off and eventually defeat their doubts by performing compulsions. It really does feel like an achievable proposition. However, unbeknownst to them, a positive feedback loop is secretly at work inside their brain. It ensures that every time they perform a compulsion, the associated doubt is fortified, returning more frequently and more aggressively thereafter. In turn, this makes the sufferer more anxious, depressed and paranoid, spawning new doubts which will follow the same pattern. Tragically, the very thing that they thought would help them, ends up hurting them instead. Left to its own devices, a sufferer's OCD will slowly get worse and worse, because they will always be inclined to switch off those unbearable alarms. Eventually their life will be consumed, as they end up bombarded at a devastating frequency by their extended family of super-charged triggers.

Ignoring the occasional peaks and troughs caused by life's ups and downs, this is certainly the pattern that my OCD followed from my teenage years through to middle-age. It started off as discrete throwaway thoughts which I could take or leave without any distress. Later it became short episodes centred around mildly distressing problems. While it was harder to brush aside, it was still manageable enough. The compulsions felt like a secret ally which helped me face up to my problems better. Gradually, the episodes became longer and more convoluted. The problems they centred on felt more distressing, and the compulsions started losing their effectiveness. Repetition and subterfuge became necessary. The increasing time and effort this required started to adversely affect my studies and my social life. I became more depressed and withdrawn. The compulsions no longer felt like a neat trick, but a humiliating burden. The tail had started to wag the dog. Eventually, it snowballed into a twenty-four seven living hell which laid waste to my life piecemeal. I was trapped, at the mercy of a monster, resentfully performing back-to-back compulsions all my waking life; like an alcoholic tramp rolling around in the gutter, taking swigs of methylated spirits just to get him through the day.

Now let's consider an imaginary scenario to illustrate a hypothetical obsession, trigger and compulsion. Janet develops an obsession about an electrical fire burning her house down while she's at work. Leaving the house for work each morning, she starts to wonder if she unplugged the appliances she just used, and whether she switched off the electrical sockets they were plugged into. This doubtful thought is the trigger. The mounting anxiety this trigger leaves her saddled with eventually becomes too much, and Janet devises a compulsion to counter it. When the trigger strikes, she goes back inside the house and checks all of the sockets she used until she's satisfied there's no threat. Then the anxiety abates and she's free to leave the house and go to work again.

If allowed to develop naturally, Janet's compulsion might graduate into checking every socket in the house instead of just those she used. Sometimes, while she's in the process of checking all of the sockets, the trigger will fire again regarding the sockets she checked first. So she'll have to repeat the process from scratch as many times as it takes to switch off the panic alarms in her mind, so that she can leave the house and go to work. In time, she may find herself returning home multiple times before she makes it to work, as the trigger keeps refiring every time she leaves the house and drives away. Further down the line, she might find the checks don't seem to be cutting it any more. So she might start switching off the electrical supply to her home every day as a final precaution before leaving for work. And when that no longer provides the necessary re-assurance, she might start loading her electrical appliances into the boot of her car every day because it's the only way that she can come close to being sure that they're not still plugged in while she's at work.

Poor old Janet took what seemed like reasonable measures to deal with an unacceptable doubt. But those measures backfired horribly, only serving to make the doubt worse and worse, until she was rendered a slave to an obsession she never wanted. This captures the insidious counter-intuitive essence of OCD.

The recommended treatment for OCD in the UK is a combination of Cognitive Behavioural Therapy(CBT) and Selective Serotonin Reuptake Inhibitor(SSRI) medication. I discuss this in greater detail in Appendix 4.

The line between OCD and Tourette syndrome is a blurry one. Both disorders involve anomalous activity in the same areas of the brain. Sufferers of one disorder, often exhibit symptoms of the other one at some point. Many people who develop OCD later on in life, report having had facial tics as children. I fall within this category myself. Moreover, in my early twenties, my mental compulsions started spilling over into physical compulsions which had all the hallmarks of Tourette syndrome. Despite these overlaps, OCD and Tourette syndrome are still officially considered to be separate disorders.

Current understanding dictates that the underlying brain processes driving OCD are the same for all OCD sufferers. However the nature of obsessions and compulsions can vary dramatically between sufferers. To reflect this, some sufferers refer to their OCD using a more specific sub-category - e.g. pure O, scrupulosity, symmetry, ROCD, HOCD, COCD ... the list goes on.

In reality, a given sufferer's OCD will likely comprise more than one of these sub-categories, usually with one becoming more dominant than the rest. Sufferers who mainly perform mental mantras in response to intrusive thoughts will say they have pure O. Those who deal mostly with contamination issues say they have COCD. People whose obsessions mostly revolve around relationships say they have ROCD, and so on.

I suspect that these sub-types evolved as a kind of shorthand for sufferers to quickly convey the nature of their obsessions and compulsions to fellow sufferers and therapists, without having to habitually regurgitate the same old spiel. I personally have no problem with it, but some psychologists and charities frown upon this practice, rightly pointing out that it can mislead people into thinking that OCD is more than one disorder. To make matters worse, some of the acronyms are used to refer to more than one sub-category, which is a little self-defeating, e.g. ROCD can mean Religious OCD or Relationship OCD.

So these concerns are clearly valid. Even so, I've found that we sufferers still tend to use the sub-categories regardless. I guess from our point of view, these terms are already cemented into the OCD vernacular, and they save us a lot of time and duplication. So, rightly or wrongly, until it's outlawed, I'll continue referring to my OCD as *pure O.*

Pure O (or purely obsessional OCD) is an unusual form of OCD. It can be tricky to identify as OCD, since the compulsions tend to play out covertly in the mind, as opposed to the overt compulsions normally associated with OCD. That's why OCD always eluded me over the years, as I intermittently sifted through all the known mental disorders, trying to find a match for my mystery problem. The definitions of OCD available during that time window only covered overt compulsions. And while I did exhibit some of those to a degree, the overwhelming source of my troubles was pure O, so those were the symptoms I based my searches on.

The term pure O is a misnomer born from the initial misconception that this was a form of OCD that didn't involve any compulsions. It was only later that it was acknowledged that the compulsions were still taking place, albeit out of sight, inside the sufferer's mind.

When I first heard the term pure O, I thought it must be a brand of orange juice or oxygen in a can. But the catchy name belies a more malignant nature. The symptoms of pure O are the same as normal OCD up to a point - i.e. frequently recurring episodes of extreme anxiety triggered by sudden uninvited false doubts or intrusive thoughts. However, when it comes to the compulsions, pure O sufferers devise mental rituals to deal with the triggers, instead of physical ones. A common approach used by pure O sufferers is using *mental mantras* to neutralise triggers.

A *mental mantra* is a set of steps that a pure O sufferer recites in their mind to disarm a trigger. A different mantra has to be tailor-made for each different trigger. They're akin to magic spells or computer programs which are gradually evolved and tweaked over time. If mentally reciting the mantra doesn't work, then it can be vocalised instead to give it added weight. Arguably though, at that point, it ceases to be pure O and becomes normal OCD, because a physical compulsion is introduced.

In my case, the way these mantras tend to work is two-fold. First, the trigger is taken to one side and broken down until it's a more manageable proposition. Then the trigger's content is carefully sifted through, ascertaining what's really true and false. The false content is disposed of along the way and the true content is preserved. It's rather like placing an infected thought in quarantine and decontaminating it.

That all probably sounds straight forward enough, but in a state of heightened anxiety, it all becomes very chaotic and treacherous. It can be remarkably tricky to pull off and repetition is often required, "until it feels right". On the bad days, even the process of performing a compulsion can spawn new triggers; sometimes manifold triggers(*see Mandelbrot Upset*). On those days, you just can't win. Everything is too slippery to get a hold of, and things constantly get switched around so that innocent thoughts suddenly become horrible unacceptable thoughts. False dependencies and associations lie in wait to ambush ordinary thoughts and spin them into repugnant nightmares ... "Ah, so if you think this, then surely it must also mean that?", "Wait, did you mean your ex-girlfriend there, or did you mean your mum?", "Are you sure you want to stroke this little dog, or were you considering breaking its neck just then?", "Were you really just praying to God for this person to get better, or were you secretly praying to The Devil for them to die?". These are the days when you truly wish there was an off switch for your brain. These are the days when you would rather not leave the house, because just managing the OCD alone is an extremely demanding full-time job, which quickly leaves you utterly exhausted and depressed. Trying to deal with that in public is impossibly hard and humiliating to boot.

Some of the most miserable experiences of my life have been trying to exorcise rampant OCD triggers in crowded supermarkets, in meetings at work, or on social outings; places where there's constant distraction and no place to hide. If you're not careful you can end up stuck in that terrible state of mind, sometimes referred to as *brain lock*; trapped in a looping nightmare with anxiety ramped up through the roof; trying and failing ad nauseam to deal with all the triggers that are accumulating. Meanwhile you're left badly treading water with whatever else is going on around you in the real world. You end up feeling extremely uncomfortable and contaminated on a spiritual level, because you inevitably end up losing track of some triggers in the throes of the multi-tasking mayhem. If you knew at the outset that it was going to turn out that way, then you'd completely avoid that situation. But you never know until it's too late. So why not just get up and leave then? Well sometimes you can't without a damn good reason. Besides, it always feels like you can beat it with just one more attempt. More importantly though, it feels like an unwise policy to just give up and abandon ship any time the going gets rough. That sets dangerous precedents which will quickly leave you completely withdrawn and unable to do any social activities. So you're always inclined to stay and fight. Unfortunately though, when it's that bad, staying and fighting does you a tremendous amount of harm. Ironically, you do end up avoiding those things as a result, and you do become more withdrawn regardless. It truly is a no win situation.

The sufferer must come across as a remarkably dour and moody individual under these circumstances. I die a little inside when I think back to weddings, parties and work outings when I was trapped in that godawful state. It could go on for hours. You pray people will just leave you alone until you've got it under control, because interruptions demolish the house of cards you're carefully trying to construct, and you have to start all over again. You start resenting interruptions because of this and it feels like people are doing it deliberately just to spite you. In that state, you're simply in no condition to be around other people. Looking back now, I dread what people must have thought of me in those moments. I remember getting home after such occasions and feeling just horrible in every way; nursing a bad head and chronic gut pains; up for hours, trying to somehow coax my mind back around into an acceptable state before going to bed; wondering why I bothered going out at all; incrementally less inclined to go out the next time an opportunity arose. And that is how it works - goodbye life, hello isolation. A very cruel disorder. You give it two hundred per cent all your waking life, and you get a very poor return indeed on that investment.

There's an element of temporary amnesia to OCD. When a trigger strikes, the certainty the sufferer normally has about the thing in question is temporarily removed, like a rug being pulled out from under them. This is particularly disturbing when it comes to the kind of intrusive thoughts which characterise pure O. These are not the kind of ideas you ever want to feel uncertain about - e.g. sexual preferences, harm, morality, memories. But no matter how convincing some of these doubts may seem at the time, in reality, none of them ever come true. By virtue of them being pure O doubts, these ideas are always anathema to the sufferer - their worst fears, abhorrent opposites of their true values and preferences. There's a subtle but crucial distinction to bear in mind here. Despite the sufferer's certainty gauge having an intermittent fault, their moral compass always remains completely intact regardless. So they would never actually act on any of these doubts. Yet this is remarkably hard for them to realise whilst in the grip of the sickening tormenting doubts. Because of the missing certainty, it really feels like their core values are hanging in the balance; like their integrity is in danger of being irreversibly corrupted if they don't take some kind of preventative action. It comes down to an unacceptable fear of "What if I loved the things I hate?" or "What if I did the worst thing I can imagine?" or "What if I was the worst kind of person I can think of?". The possibility is so bitterly unpalatable, that the sufferer feels overwhelmingly obliged to re-establish complete certainty that these things are not possible after all. Alas, that kind of certainty can be incredibly elusive in the mind of an OCD sufferer who's just been triggered. And that's roughly when the trouble starts.

If any of this sounds like it ought to be unnecessary or avoidable, then I'm afraid I'm not explaining myself very well. You're just going to have to take my word for it when I tell you that it is not. Not by a long shot. It's more compelling than crack cocaine, and harder to kick. If OCD were avoidable, I would have happily left it far behind when it first reared its head. God knows I've strained beyond my natural limits countless times to try and extricate myself from the clutches of this humiliating life-sucking curse. I've tried to beat it, to outrun it, to roll with the punches, to shrug it off. I've tried every new approach I can think of along the way - defiance, aggressive control, serene control, refusal to engage, avoiding triggers, seeking triggers out, sarcasm, making fun of it ... all to no avail. And that shines a light on the very nature of OCD - you simply do not get to make that choice. The harder you fight, the more logic you throw at it, the worse it gets. Always. End of. Imagine, if you will, a Chinese finger trap, which tightens more and more every time you try to wriggle out of it. That is the essence of OCD. Every single intuitive action you take to fight it or escape it, counter-intuitively draws you in deeper until you are absolutely beholden to it. It's one of the rare areas in life where courage, defiance and tenacity are cynically punished.

It's only when you understand the true nature of OCD better, that you can try and change the game and manage it a different way. Then it becomes more about counter-intuitively resisting triggers, passivity, non-engagement, taking a leap of faith and forcing yourself to go left when everything screams "GO RIGHT!". And that is a remarkably hard feat to pull off, let me tell you. ERP looks lovely on paper, but what it really boils down to is quitting your compulsions cold turkey. Meanwhile, you've got to suck up the unbearable discomfort that leaves you with until your obsessions slowly loosen their grip. The trouble with that is, it's only a matter of short time until you have a bad day with your OCD, and an absolute doozy of a trigger comes along that you really feel you cannot live with despite what the textbooks say. That being the case, I think this kind of therapy can only ever be a messy "two steps forward, one step back" kind of deal, with lots of guaranteed failures along the way. Nevertheless, under the right circumstances, and with enough blind courage and persistence, it can be used to gradually wean sufferers off their current compulsions.

Ultimately, I suspect there is only so much proselytising sufferers can do, and OCD is something that has to be experienced first-hand to be believed. I have often wondered if I would take OCD seriously if I didn't have it myself. Honestly, I don't think I even want to know the answer to that question. This is why I try to be as patient as possible when people get it wrong, or make jokes, or don't take it seriously. Why should they understand it? I barely understand it myself and I've got it. Besides, being too precious about it isn't going to give anyone a better understanding. More likely they'll just think people with OCD are stuck up and touchy, without a sense of humour. That said, it can be hard not to bite when celebrities casually misappropriate your waking nightmare to score low-hanging pathos points with the media, or when people use it as a lazy comedy trope to get cheap laughs. That's a big ask.

This thing is constantly underestimated and misrepresented in the media. They're intent on making it a casual throwaway foible or quirk. A fashion accessory you can claim to have for a while because it sounds edgy, then ditch when you're bored of it. I've seen a world famous footballer, a champion cage fighter, and several highly successful actors all claim that they have OCD. And maybe they do, but I'd like to know what kind of OCD they have when it allows them to rise to those dizzy competitive heights in the public eye. Because that's the kind of OCD I want, but it's sure as hell not the kind that I've got!

So what? Why care? Why not laugh it off? Let it go. Live and let live. Well, unfortunately there's a bigger problem here. It's highly likely that people with OCD will be unemployed at some point as a result of their disorder. Maybe multiple times. Therefore they're likely to have to interface with welfare services. As someone who's been through this experience in the UK in 2016, I can tell you that those people do not take OCD very seriously at all. You have a hell of a battle on your hands convincing them otherwise. The media misrepresentation of OCD and its misappropriation by celebrities does not serve you well when you're in that position. It muddies the playing field and gives the welfare services and their shills carte blanche to dismiss OCD as a throwaway quirk not to be taken seriously. Something people can live with and achieve amazing success in spite of. Unfortunately it is all too serious to the people who've lost everything to it - their jobs, their partners, their savings, their minds, their lives.

If you don't have OCD, then you need to know that there's a secret order of people out there who are living this nightmare for real. They're most likely sworn to silence. You won't see them in any magazine articles or on any talk shows. You work alongside them. You sit next to them on the train. You pass them in the supermarket. You are their mother, their brother, their lover, their friend. And you will likely never know unless they volunteer it, because they're working undercover on pain of death. But they're out there, and they are legion, and believe me when I tell you that they deserve your empathy; or failing that, the benefit of the doubt. No pun intended.

Appendix 2 - My Journey with OCD

I have a type of OCD sometimes referred to as *pure O*. It's a less publicised form of the disorder whereby mental rituals are carried out instead of the physical rituals normally associated with OCD.

It's rarely a black and white split though, and while the lion's share of my OCD is pure O, I do still exhibit some physical symptoms too. For instance:

- I often get stuck locking doors or switching things off. I'm compelled to repeat the action until the penny drops that the door is really locked or the thing is really off.

- I'm prone to skin picking(dermatillomania) and skin biting (dermatophagia).

- Some physical and vocal gestures have been known to accompany my pure O rituals over the years.

- I often go a little overboard on cleaning. I can happily make an evening's washing up stretch to two hours without even trying. And that's without the drying.

- I have a few other physical overspills regarding contamination and perfectionism.

For many OCD sufferers, physical symptoms like this manifest to a devastating degree. Yet for some reason, they only affect me relatively mildly, and the overwhelming focus of my OCD is pure O.

I didn't always know that I had OCD though. For the longest time I lived in ignorance. But while I didn't have a name for it, I knew something was wrong. A lifetime of comparing my behaviour with other people's, gradually threw a lot of tins of paint over an invisible problem. A fundamental difference between how I processed things, and how they did. There was a spanner in the works. I kept getting snagged on certain problem situations which I couldn't get past. Impasses which I didn't seek out, yet which found me regardless. They were taking me out of a game I badly needed to be in and making me fail when I needed to succeed. I had to believe I could get on top of it all and be like everyone else. I eventually learned to try and limit the damage by rationalising through the problem, then taking it on again with a more positive mindset. I thought I was pretty good at that too - conjuring lemonade out of lemons, making the best of a bad lot.

But the strangest thing started to happen. Even after going through that laborious process, I was finding that my new resolve was evaporating away remarkably quickly. Like winning at Snakes n' Ladders, only to slide all the way back down to the bottom of the board on a hidden snake. It didn't seem fair. I was finding myself pinned down under heavy fire again far too soon to achieve anything. I was trying really hard to be brave but I simply wasn't being allowed to face up to my fears. Something was sabotaging my best efforts. Whenever it happened, I didn't know what else to do except brush myself off, go back to the beginning, and start building my fragile house of cards again from scratch. But after you've done it enough times, you already know what's coming next. That's when it starts to get really interesting. And by interesting, I mean horrific ... my life given over to a clandestine civil war; lost inside myself, fighting, struggling; trying to defy the enemy inside who was gradually consuming me; trying to find new imaginative ways of putting it down; so many epic would-be final battles; so much hope and courage frittered away in vain. But by God, it absolutely would not be put down. I always wound up right back at the start of the board again. A very cruel situation to be in.

All I could do was keep moving forward in spite of it, in desperate hope that I would somehow find a way to overcome it one day. As childhood gave way to adulthood, things got very messy indeed and big cracks started to appear. I was in a lot of trouble.

There's still much debate over whether OCD is a genetic hand-me-down, a random brain anomaly, a product of learned behaviour, or maybe even the result of a virus. I can't say for sure, but in my case, I suspect it was inherited; always there, lurking, lying dormant in the shadows; just waiting for the right fuel to come within reach, so it could light up and take centre stage.

For about as far back as I can remember, I frequently got stuck on certain things. Ideas, thoughts, words or phrases which didn't seem to pack the required meaning somehow. So I'd be moved to go back and repeat them in my mind until they did. In the beginning, it didn't cause me distress as such, but nonetheless, I felt obliged to do it. Like scratching an itch.

Going to secondary school was like giving OCD rocket fuel. My first recollection of a discernible sustained episode of pure O OCD was when I was twelve years old. I was terrified of reading out loud in English classes. My English teacher was quick to spot the problem, and made damn sure that I read out in class all the time after that. Who knows - maybe she thought it might help me conquer my fear, but alas it did not. It was a humiliating ordeal which I dreaded all week long. I was so preoccupied with the resulting anxiety, that I wasn't focussing on the books we were meant to be studying, and I wasn't learning anything during those lessons, or even the ones preceding them.

The feelings were simply too much to bear, and I unwittingly started devising a mental routine which I would run through in the time leading up to the lessons. It was a last ditch hope to tie a tourniquet around the panic, and get me into a better frame of mind to face the fear. It seemed to help at first, but eventually it stopped working, and things started going the other way again. So I would redouble my efforts and go through the routine as many times as it took, trying to make my intention more earnest every time so that it would stick better. But it never lasted long regardless, and the fear always came back stronger and sooner than before. Things spiralled out of control and I ended up an embarrassing basket case in those English lessons. I could hardly breathe and I could hear my own voice trembling audibly among the sniggering of the other children. This was fertile hunting ground indeed for OCD. It would be a regular feature in my life after that.

Around that time, my family started attending church regularly. I found that sometimes when I tried to pray, the most unwanted blasphemous thoughts would pop into my head out of nowhere. Given the religious context, this troubled me deeply, and I started to wonder if I was possessed. I was eventually moved to ask my mum about it. She said it was probably the Devil trying to trick me by planting bad ideas in my head. Honestly, if I was in her shoes, I think I'd have said exactly the same thing. And in a way, she was absolutely right!

Thanks to some tough years at school, my OCD graduated into the big leagues. For a while, I got my first taste of what it was like to live with OCD around the clock without any days off. Last thing at night, first thing in the morning, and with a punishing frequency throughout the day. Needless to say, it interfered with my studies and my exam results started taking a nose dive. The combined effect of everything left me very depressed. I hoped it would automatically go away after school ended, but alas, it followed me to university. Thankfully, it was no longer the full-time nightmare it had been at school. It settled down into a more episodic pattern, with some ad hoc residual stuff in between. But ebbs and flows notwithstanding, OCD had one foot inside the door now and it wasn't going anywhere any time soon.

New obsessions started to emerge about security and conflict situations. These obsessions would remain a constant thread throughout my journey with OCD, but they were particularly rife during my time at university and for some years thereafter. Wherever I was, I needed to feel like I was ready to deal with anything bad that could possibly happen. This was especially relevant if I was going out somewhere. So before I left home, I'd take some time to psyche myself up, performing various mental rituals to re-assure myself. If I tried going out without doing that, I was left with this unbearable feeling of being naked and vulnerable, like a balloon walking out into a world of pins. When done right though, that routine felt like putting on a magic suit of armour, and it could put me in a good mood for the duration of the outing. As time went on however, it became increasingly difficult to do it right, and even when I pulled it off, it never lasted very long anyway. Without a viable alternative, all I could do was keep going through the routine again and again in my mind until the bad feelings finally went away. But this could take an awfully long time and entire outings were frequently given over to endless cycles of rumination. My magic suit of armour had become a cursed ball and chain.

OCD caused me many such social problems at university. When a trigger strikes, your confidence instantly evaporates and you're left in an uptight distant state of mind until you can get it under control again. And no matter how hard you try to conceal it, experience has taught me that it doesn't exactly endear you to the people you're around at the time. Inevitably it leads to a lot of dead air, negative body language and botched interactions. Most people pick up on these bad vibes, misinterpret them as moodiness or hostility, and give you a wide berth after that.

While I was at university, I started self-medicating with alcohol and tobacco. Alcohol tended to take the edge off my OCD, making it easier to deal with. Now, many sufferers say their OCD gets worse when they drink or when they're hungover, but for some reason it tends to go the other way with me, or at least it doesn't make any difference. As for the smoking, it helped in various ways. For one, it was like a rip cord I could pull to extricate myself from tricky situations; like whenever OCD was too much to deal with in company, or whenever there was a trigger I needed to get away from. It was also a way of rewarding myself for successfully completing my compulsions. Like an OCD punctuation mark drawing a line under the episode and turning a clean sheet. But all things considered, I could never in good conscience recommend either of these things to help with OCD or anything else. The health risks are widely documented, and whatever they may appear to give you in one hand, they take back with interest out of the other. But back then for me, they were just socially acceptable life jackets which were hard for a drowning man not to grab onto and wear.

When university ended, my OCD kicked into high gear again. I knew I'd screwed up my degree, and I developed a pathological fear about leaving university. I didn't have a clue what I was supposed to do next, and there weren't exactly a lot of options available for someone with a poor degree anyway. It would be great seeing family and friends again, but there were also some negative connotations attached to going home again - like returning to the scene of a crime. Regardless, I was in debt and lacked a plan B or the cunning to conjure one up out of thin air. So I resigned myself to going home and taking refuge in low paid casual work for a while.

I started developing some very strange physical compulsions around this time. From my point of view, I don't think the mental rituals were really cutting the mustard any more. So it felt both natural and necessary to augment them with physical gestures to make up for the shortfall - the belt and braces approach so to speak. I would perform both together "until it felt right". There's a close relationship between OCD and Tourette syndrome, and these gestures were certainly testament to that.

Among the gestures I remember were:

- vocalising certain key words or phrases from my pure O mantras.

- facial gestures, like hard blinking, or opening my mouth painfully wide.

- hand movements, usually together with a word or phrase.

- banging myself hard on the head, or squeezing my head tightly in my hands.

- slamming my head forwards and down, as if to bang my brain against the wall of my skull.

- making a clicking or popping sound with my tongue at the back of my mouth.

- taking massive breaths and holding them in until I got a head buzz and almost passed out.

- and my personal favourite: an extreme grin, where I bit my teeth hard together and scrunched my face up into an exaggerated pained smile. To me, it felt like I was purging the contents of my brain by squeezing a clenched fist around it. I'd do this with such force, my whole head would start shaking.

I tried very hard to keep all of this private, for obvious reasons(!), but it started to get away from me eventually. Performing these compulsions any place where other people are coming and going is always going to be a risky business. But I think there's an aspect to OCD whereby you believe you're hiding your compulsions better than you really are. You have to believe that really or you'd never leave the house. So it was only a matter of time until I got caught with my pants down. Here are some fairly horrifying examples I can remember:

- The night before my girlfriend's degree ceremony, we were staying in a nearby hotel together. We were getting ready to go out for a meal. I got stuck in the bathroom, frantically trying to get a handle on some slippery OCD triggers which were bombarding me. I knew I'd been an unusually long time but I just had to get it under control before I could face anything else. She overheard me making the tongue-clicking sound in my throat, and banged on the door, asking why I was "clucking like a chicken".

- Some months after that, we went for a meal with two old university friends. Once again, I was getting swamped by some nasty triggers and was struggling to keep a lid on it all. As I was furtively performing my compulsions, her old friend suddenly turned to me and asked why I was making that strange sound with my throat.

- Around that same time, I was working as a night porter at a local hotel. There was a pretty receptionist who I got on really well with. I turned up for work one night and, as usual, went straight into the kitchen to make a cup of tea. Nobody else was in there so when a trigger came calling, I felt free to augment the necessary compulsion with that ridiculous extreme grin. In the midst of my bizarre incantation, I suddenly noticed the receptionist walking into the kitchen towards me. I think the spectacle totally freaked her out, because she simply turned around and walked right back out again. We never spoke about it. I desperately wanted to say something to her about it, but I didn't even know how to explain it to her. I was left wondering what she made of it and whom else she might've told(see Reverse Engineering Mega-Doubt).

When you don't even know you've got a condition, let alone the name of it, it's really hard to know what to say to people under those circumstances. No one wants to look creepy or crazy. So if it were up to you, you'd never do any of that when other people were around, but sometimes you just don't get a say in that. So you kid yourself that you're employing enough subterfuge to cover it up. When you get caught out unexpectedly though, there are no words for how devastatingly humiliating it feels. How do you even explain that? What could you possibly say to make it OK? How are you supposed to face that person again with your head held high?

I used to find quitting jobs to be quite an effective way of culling obsessions, as inevitably many of them would centre around work. This definitely contributed to my quitting the hotel job, as my OCD was getting out of control towards the end of that. Apparently it didn't respond well to working alone at night in an unpredictable, overworked environment, which was fast becoming the car theft Mecca of my home town. Who knew!

But no sooner had I started my next job, than a whole new glut of obsessions and compulsions started slowly coming out of the woodwork to replace the old ones. To make matters worse, a spate of burglaries where I lived left me saddled with insomnia, paranoia and some new checking compulsions. While the worst of my OCD was still confined to temporary episodes, they were happening more frequently and more intensely. On top of that, there was a steadily rising tide of background OCD to deal with in between the episodes. It was getting really old now.

Only a few months into the next job, OCD was firing on all cylinders again. Around this time, I started noticing some new physical symptoms. Whenever OCD was most active, I'd get pains around my gut area, and a headache in the front right-hand region of my brain. The combined effect was very debilitating and could persist long after the OCD had died down. I'd invariably get home from work feeling ill, after a day of trying to do my job, while defusing the barrage of grenades OCD was hurling at me. Nursing my aching head and gut, I'd collapse in a heap and remain there all evening, trying to rein in the OCD and recover from the day's beating. When it gets that bad, you really need those evenings to recuperate enough to entertain the idea of going back the next day and doing it all over again. Literally good for nothing else, I did my best to avoid clubs, social outings, and other people in general. It's not so much a choice as a necessity.

Up until this point, I don't ever recall acknowledging the OCD as a problem that I needed to address. It just felt like an eccentric aspect of my internal struggle; a private demon I needed to grapple with until I got the upper hand. But I never regarded it as a mental health problem that I needed to get help with. I think that was partly due to my own ignorance, and partly due to the fact that people in England simply didn't talk in those terms back then. From my perspective, it felt like an invisible threshold was crossed at some point during the mid 1990s. After that it suddenly became OK to discuss such things in the media, and that subsequently trickled down into wider society. New terms started to enter the vernacular, like depression, therapy, and anti-depressants. Before that, it felt like people either "just got on with it" in spite of their problems, or had a nervous breakdown and disappeared for a while. It was only after this threshold was crossed that I started looking at my problem in a different light and considering my options.

Increasingly unsure how to control it, and worried about my future, I finally went to the doctor in 1997. I'd been really reluctant to do this, because it felt like crossing the Rubicon; like a one-way ticket from sanity over to insanity; like coming out of the closet as a crazy person. But I was desperate, and I'd had enough of trying to think my way out of this impossible puzzle. So I decided I was going to get to the bottom of it once and for all. I made out a very thorough list of all my symptoms, detailing the themes I became obsessed about, the recurring anxiety they induced, and the mantras I recited to make it temporarily stop. It was worth humiliating myself in front of my doctor to finally find out what was wrong with me and get some help with it.

A couple of perfunctory questions later, he gave me a drive-thru diagnosis of clinical depression. No apparent process, no psychologist, no second opinion, nothing. I had more faith in doctors back then so I didn't even think to question it. He wrote me out a prescription for Prozac, allaying my concerns with a delightful little quip about it being so harmless that people in the USA had Prozac parties.

In retrospect it was like visiting a bad Santa Claus in a department store grotto. Glibly going through the motions, pretending to listen, nodding in all the right places. Then half-heartedly handing over the same cheap inappropriate gift that he gave all the other children he didn't care about. The poor kid thinks it's really him. Then he's left confused on the way home when he opens up some naff plastic puzzle that he never even asked for in his letter.

And while his diagnosis was not entirely wrong, it totally missed the fundamental problem I'd gone there to get help with in the first place. I certainly don't want to downplay how serious depression can be. Some people are plagued with it to a horribly debilitating degree, the likes of which I've never experienced. In my particular case though, the depression I've experienced has been a lot easier to manage than the OCD I've experienced. There's an unrelenting treacherous self-sabotaging aspect to the OCD that's absent from the depression. It's like being forced to play chess with the Devil every five minutes. You quickly grow sick and tired of the fiendish difficulty and the endless repetition. You absolutely do not want to play any more. But you have to keep playing regardless. For the rest of your life.

I kept going back to the doctor and explaining that the pills weren't making a dent in my problem. He would just increase the dosage or switch the brand like it was nothing. I eventually asked if I could see somebody more qualified in matters of mental health. So he referred me to a psychologist. I went and explained all of my symptoms to the psychologist, just as I'd done with the doctor. Unbelievably, he just backed up the doctor's lazy diagnosis, and put me on a different SSRI. I was so disappointed. I went back a couple of times to explain that the pills weren't helping with my problem. Like the doctor before him, he just upped doses and changed brands until I was on an "elephant strength" SSRI. My blinkered pharmaceutical safari continued.

Perhaps it wasn't their fault. Perhaps they hadn't heard about pure O OCD back then. Perhaps there was no textbook entry to refer to. I don't know. All I do know is that I found my experience with them incredibly frustrating and misleading. A crucial opportunity was missed and I ended up in limbo for a long time as a result.

I was getting sick of taking pills which didn't even help me with my problem, but left me with some unpleasant side effects instead; including lucid nightmares, decreased libido, a swollen tongue, a dry mouth, and the inability to cry(*see The Onion Field*).

I became very disillusioned with the medical establishment, and decided to ditch the pills and go it alone; intent on redoubling my efforts and beating this thing with the power of my mind alone. A rather unfortunate choice given the dynamics of OCD, i.e. the harder you try to control it, the more it ends up controlling you. But of course, I didn't know any of this at the time. It felt like the intuitive thing to do, indeed the only thing to do, was to try and get it under control using the only means at my disposal: my mind.

By the way - never come off an "elephant strength" SSRI cold. I was subjected to a series of sudden violent head buzzes over the fortnight that followed. Like massive electric shocks shooting through my brain without any warning. I genuinely thought I was not long for this world. It woke me up to just how potent these pills really are. That, together with the nasty side effects, made me extremely reluctant to go anywhere near SSRIs ever again.

Blown around upon the vagaries of life and work, my OCD had continued to follow an episodic pattern up until this point. There were pretty intense nightmare periods, but there were also occasional grace periods - often when jobs ended or circumstances somehow changed for the better. When you've got OCD though, there will always be something that comes along to fuel it regardless. Of that I'm absolutely certain. At this point though, my OCD took a major turn for the worse, catalysed by an unfortunate cocktail of inclement circumstances. It became a full time occupation and roughly ten years of living hell ensued.

My pure O tends to gravitate towards awkward conflict situations. Such themes dominated this period, with a lot of aggravation in and out of work. Since leaving university I'd been in a long-distance relationship with my girlfriend in London. I'd tried really hard to start a career down there so that I could be with her. It kept going wrong though. I'd do rounds of interviews and assessments and eventually land a graduate job. Later, that job would be withdrawn before the start date for no reason whatsoever, and I'd be back at square one. When I finally did get a job down in London, I was made redundant within just two years. Despite trying my heart out, I simply could not get another job down there. So I very reluctantly went back home again and looked for work there. I ended up in a job I never wanted but felt obliged to take. I quickly came to loathe the job and tried to get out of it. I applied for a staggering amount of jobs during that time, but just couldn't get anything suitable. I was stuck there for nine years in total. I hated some of the colleagues and managers I had to work with, and they hated me right back. All high octane fuel for OCD of course.

During that time, I passed my driving test and started driving to work. I thought driving would improve my life. I didn't see it coming but for some reason, OCD and driving went together like bullets and guns. I think it probably came down to a combination of things: a nightmarish commute across a gridlocked city, the exquisite difficulty of performing compulsions whilst driving, my dad abruptly quitting driving and assuming I would take up the slack, and the ridiculous amount of problems I had with my first car.

My dad had been a hoarder since the early 1980s but it was getting worse every passing year. The house was falling into a state of alarming disrepair as a result. On top of that, he was becoming increasingly verbally and mentally abusive. He would explode in fits of vitriolic rage whenever anybody so much as mentioned anything about the house, the hoarding or indeed the abuse. This made for an unavoidably acrimonious relationship between us which has only worsened since.

Inevitably, I lost my long-distance girlfriend down in London, and I found that difficult to handle. In retrospect though, I'm amazed she held on as long as she did. Even so, I became extremely depressed after this. I felt like I'd failed to get on top of my problems and secure a good career. I felt like I'd lost everything. I felt absolutely lost and I was catching hell on all sides.

Fuelled by all these stressors, OCD was no longer confined to discrete episodes with relatively normal periods in between. It had become a permanent burden I secretly had to carry around with me everywhere I went. There was no escape. It was a way of life now. I had to multi-task all day long, every day. It was too much, juggling work and social activities on top of it, and something had to give. I gradually retreated into myself to limit my exposure to triggers, and to allow enough downtime to recover for work. I took whatever alone time I could get my hands on. It was like opium to me.

Something new started happening. As usual, obsessions would start up about a root problem, developing a bunch of triggers along the way. But then later, if left to ferment long enough, secondary triggers would start to evolve, then tertiary ones and so on. These were indirect associations to the primary obsession. Often words in my case, though not always. But taking words as an example, it would start off with a word directly related to the main obsession. Then later, words related to that word would become triggers. Next, words which formed compound words with any of those words became triggers. Later still, words that sounded like any of those words became triggers.

These word farms were in constant flux and varied in depth, but I'll take a hypothetical example to an extreme here just to illustrate how bad it could get in theory:

- original trigger: table

- related words: desk, bench, counter, chair, legs, wood

- compound words: (table-)football, (table-)cloth, (table-)manners, dinner(-table), times(-table), water(-table), (desk-)drawer, (desk-)lamp, (desk-)tidy, news(-desk), foreign(-desk), hot(-desk), sports(-desk), (bench-)press, (bench-)mark, work(-bench), (counter-)weight, (counter-)measures, (counter-)intuitive, (counter-)strike, Geiger(-counter), shop(-counter), bean(-counter), (chair-)lift, (chair-)man, high(-chair), office(-chair), arm(-chair), (legs-)eleven, hairy(-legs), dog(-legs), chicken(-legs), (wood-)smoke, (wood-)saw, (wood-)axe, (wood-)shed, (wood-)grain, sandal(-wood), hard(-wood), soft(-wood), fire(-wood)

- sound-a-like words(just using table, or the list would be ridiculously long!): label, cable, fable, able, stable, sable, Babel, Abel, Mable, Betty Grable, ladle, cradle, bagel, finagle

I'm sure you get the picture. Now like I said, that's an extreme example, and in reality I'd be looking at a smaller subset of that for each trigger. Still, I shudder when I recall just how many of these I gradually accumulated, and the cruel futility of trying to deal with them. Before too long, I found myself servicing this vast labyrinthine menagerie of triggers related to my obsessions. It got absolutely insane. OCD's fishing net was so ubiquitously cast, that I could barely move before I got tangled up in triggers and compulsions. I had to become very good at multi-tasking. I had to become an actor, a conjurer, an escape artist, a bullshit artist. And that latter aspect crucified me. I hate lying, but I was trapped in an impossible situation. So it was either that or talk about my problem honestly with people, and I wasn't ready to do that. I didn't even know what I was supposed to say to them about it. It wasn't like anything I'd ever heard of. They'd just think I was a creepy crazy weirdo and I'd probably get fired or taken away by the men in white coats.

There was only so much covering up I could do though, and it all became too much. I had to stop reading books in my free time because the triggers made it a miserable, torturous experience. Every time OCD struck, I'd have to perform the necessary compulsions then re-read the last sentence/paragraph/page to get the thread back again. I tried to battle through it but I'd have to stop and do this so frequently, that it completely defeated the object. I'd be forced to retreat after some hours, feeling quite unwell, having badly read half a page or less. I am not exaggerating about that either. For the same reason, I had to stop listening to music with words in, and I gave my TV away. I refused to give up watching DVDs though. And boy, did I pay dearly for that. I don't know what my record was but I regularly recall making two hour films stretch to five hours. It really wasn't worth the pain or the time hit, but somehow it felt like an important escape at the time.

Work, with its emails, documents, manuals and conversations became a huge problem for me, although the kind of boring technical stuff I was working on tended to be a much less fertile hunting ground for OCD than external stimuli. Even so, there was enough to keep me busy all day long. Such was the extent of my OCD. I just had to suck it all up and multi-task the best I could, shoehorning in my compulsions wherever and however I could. Although in retrospect, I was usually shoehorning the work in around the compulsions by that stage.

Living on coffee, cigarettes, alcohol and woefully inadequate sleep, I brought all of my available resources to bear upon this most formidable adversary. I ended up feeling tired and ill most of the time. It's a very special kind of private hell that I would not wish on anyone(who I liked).

I still tried to kid myself that I was concealing the problem with stealth and subterfuge - using sleight of hand to cleverly subsume it all into whatever I happened to be doing at the time. At some point during all this, I attended a relative's wedding. I remember that I was having a terrible day with OCD that day. Normally I'd try to get it squared away before attending something like that. Sure the OCD would soon come on again, but it would buy me some time and put a better complexion on the day somehow. But that day, it just wasn't happening and I had triggers coming out of my ears. We arrived at the wedding late and the only seats left were directly behind the bride and groom so we had to sit there. I can still remember grappling with the OCD during the ceremony, feeling very exposed and uncomfortable. But still, I was confident that I was sufficiently concealing my inner drama from the outside world. Months later, the groom's parents visited my mum and dad. They were playing them back a video of the wedding ceremony. I heard laughter coming from the room they were in, so I went to find out what the joke was. Well, it turned out I was the joke - they remarked how funny I looked on the video because I was acting all agitated, pulling strange faces, and looking around a lot. That was a hell of a low point for me. I became extremely self-conscious after that, and thought twice before showing my face in public. I'd been foolish to believe that I was hiding it all that time. I was slowly losing myself, and I didn't like the weird person I was becoming instead. It made me very sad.

I noticed another change during this period. Previously, obsessions tended to evaporate fairly quickly once the thing driving them was removed from my life. That was no longer necessarily the case. Obsessions could quite happily perpetuate beyond that now, living on through vestigial triggers which had been burned into my brain for so long that they'd become second nature. The gift that keeps on giving. In fact, I still find myself servicing triggers that were spawned over ten years ago from problems that are long gone now. It makes no earthly sense, but they've become part of how my waking mind works. Involuntary functions like blinking or breathing. They're almost like wormholes through space and time. Placeholders hard-wired back to the original thing that caused me so much distress.

I think my OCD reached its peak around 2008. That year, I had to go down to London to do two training courses for work. I tried to be positive about it and make it a good experience, but it quickly scared me how much I was struggling with everything. In the day, I found it too overwhelming trying to follow the fast-paced IT training courses while juggling a constant barrage of OCD. It left me feeling absolutely destroyed of an evening. I so badly wanted to be excited that I was in London; to get out and do stuff, see stuff, to go and see old friends and family who lived in London. But I was simply way too ill to take any of that on. This failure left me feeling so ashamed of myself. To prove to myself that I wasn't a total failure, I forced myself to do a couple of easier activities which didn't directly involve other people. I went to see a film in Leicester Square one night and I went to The British Museum after the course finished early on the last day. But those two things were so broken up and dominated by OCD that it really defeated the object. And that's exactly why you start avoiding things like that - you already know exactly how it will turn out despite your best intentions. The rest of my time was divided up between staying in my hotel room dealing with OCD, popping downstairs for unenjoyable cigarettes, and eating in the hotel restaurant. The restaurant was beyond dire, and I really wanted to go further afield because I was in London and I was on expenses. Perhaps just across the street to the pizza restaurant. But I just couldn't bring myself to do it. I knew that I would be on show and may well start acting visibly weird. It's easier to conceal that when you're with someone else, but on your own you stick out like a sore thumb. People expect less of you in a hotel restaurant somehow, and besides, that one was always empty so it was a no-brainer for me. Those training courses were a really low point for me. I realised I was in big trouble in life, and I hadn't got a clue how to get out of it. I felt very depressed around this time. I didn't know what else to do other than keep dealing with it the only way I knew how to - i.e. keep secretly squaring away all the bad stuff, and keep carrying on like everything was OK. But things were so patently not OK. I was living a lie.

I somehow managed to hold onto my job by cutting everything else out of my life, by putting in a lot of overtime to make up for the time lost to OCD, and by numbing my mind with alcohol and cigarettes on a daily basis. Obviously that comes at a shocking personal cost though. I was an absolute dribbling mess by the end of it - perpetually exhausted and miserable from carrying out non-stop compulsions to satisfy pure O's insatiable appetite. All those years of anxiety had left me with ulcerative colitis, and I was regularly experiencing some worrying pains in my chest and down my left arm. You tend to neglect your physical health when plagued with unbearable mental problems.

Eventually, the company closed and I was made redundant. I reacted to this with a kind of cognitive dissonance - half relieved that I was finally going to be extricated from this accursed job which had been the source of so much misery for me. But also terrified because I was more uncertain than I had ever been in my life about my future. I was so frazzled after all those years burning the candle at both ends, that I urgently needed a complete break. I just couldn't stand it all any more. Besides, I'd lost all confidence in my ability to handle a new work situation under those humiliating and impossible circumstances. I knew that cracks would very quickly start to emerge, and I wouldn't even know what to tell the new employer ... "Yeah, sorry for lying through my teeth in the interview and claiming I could do the job when I clearly can't! Oh yeah and by the way I'm completely stark raving BONKERS!".

So I figured I'd take a three to six month break to try and get a handle on this thing, then get back to work when I was feeling better. This strategy had worked for me in the past when the OCD got out of hand. Only this time, the break didn't seem to be helping at all. I promptly lost my girlfriend which sent me into a spiral of depression. Once again, it was really no surprise given the state I was in, but I really liked her and it hurt like hell regardless. When things started properly unravelling, I decided to attend a retreat in Peru where they administered a shamanic plant medicine called ayahuasca. I'd heard from lots of different sources how it could give you a complete mental reboot, which was exactly what I needed. I was sceptical about some of the claims, but it was my only hope at that point, and I badly needed to believe in it. So I threw myself into it.

Well, hell of a funny story - it turns out ayahuasca and pure O OCD don't play so well together. Some of the ceremonies weren't so bad actually, but when it went wrong, it really went wrong. I fainted one night while trying to stumble out of the ceremonial hut to use the toilet. To put it politely, I lost control of my bodily functions in the process. Locked in an oafish comatose tailspin, I had to be carried out like a grotesque new bride, by an intern who looked like Tarzan. Sometimes, the phrase "low point" just doesn't quite cut it. The fact is, I was overcome with mental exhaustion and gut pains from lying there for hours impotently trying to process quick-fire OCD under the influence of a drug which made that nigh impossible. You really need to keep a clear mind when taking ayahuasca. God knows I tried with all my heart, but when OCD is bad, it's simply not something you can reason with or switch off. During another ceremony, I became fairly convinced I was in Hell, and it was probably the scariest experience of my life. I found myself locked inside a toilet hut, high as a kite, and trapped inside a turbo-charged looping mind at the mercy of non-stop OCD triggers. I was no longer really aware of my identity or what I was doing there. And I was without my usual go-to compulsions to snap me out of it all. I started loudly vocalising all of my thoughts as they came into my head, much to the consternation of the people trying to run the retreat, and much to the amusement of the people attending the retreat. I can still remember the laughter from the ceremonial hut next door. I don't blame them either - I was being really loud and making an absolute jackass of myself. It was so humiliating having to face those people again after that, but I had to because I was stuck in the middle of the jungle with them until the end of the retreat.

So that was money well spent. I came back from Peru, inconsolably despondent, and resumed my spiral of depression with renewed gusto. I'd foolishly hung a lot of hopes on ayahuasca, and now I was left back at square one, and roughly £2,500 worse off. My mental problems felt worse than ever on the back of a violating drug-addled two week ordeal, which in retrospect was way too ambitious given my state of mind at the time. I stupidly started beating myself up for allowing a cure to slip through my fingers. I was stuck, and drifting out to sea without a plan B.

Some weeks later, I was nonchalantly surfing the internet in my usual depressed malaise. Clicking from video to video, looking for nothing in particular, I stumbled on a YouTube video which some kindly pure O sufferer had made to educate people about their disorder, and just like that ...

DING!

DING!!

DING!!!

DING!!!!

DING!!!!!

DING!!!!!!

... bells started going off one after another inside my head, as I realised that this thing they were describing, was exactly what I'd been living with undiagnosed all of my adult life. It was too much to take in. Prior to this, I had gradually reached the conclusion that I must be a one-off, a freak, a weirdly damaged person. Perhaps even cursed by some god I didn't believe in, or some voodoo I didn't understand. After so long on my own, it was utterly sublime discovering my private affliction had a name, and that other people had it too. I didn't even feel particularly uplifted; just completely numb, incredulous, and not sure how I was supposed to feel about it after all that time. Almost like it was too damn late to be of any use. Like a cruel consolation prize. I don't feel like I ever properly processed this revelation if I'm absolutely honest.

Infuriatingly, I'd scoured the internet many times in the ten years leading up to this, trying to match my symptoms up to known medical conditions. Certain behavioural overlaps, like obsessive cleaning and re-checking locked doors, had led me to consider OCD as a contender on more than one occasion. But the definitions available at the time only covered physical compulsions, with no mention of mental rituals. Since those mental rituals were the overwhelming source of my problems, I was always reluctantly forced to dismiss OCD as a possible cause.

At some point I watched a film called The Aviator, about the life of Howard Hughes. There were a few moments in that film which eerily echoed my problem. The most striking one was where he freezes up near the end of the film, repeating the phrase "The way of the future". This was something that I was intimately familiar with. I regularly got stuck on words and phrases which I felt obliged to repeat over and over until the meaning felt right. I'd repeat them secretly in my mind if I was in public, and verbally if I was in private. So that scene sent shivers down my spine. I researched Howard Hughes online to find out what condition he had, in hope that we shared a common problem. However, there was no mention of OCD, and my symptoms didn't match whatever condition they supposed he might have had. So likewise, I reluctantly had to close down this line of enquiry. Of course, even if OCD had been mentioned under Howard Hughes, I'd still have been forced to dismiss it, because mental rituals weren't mentioned in the OCD definitions available at the time. So I was doomed to ignorance one way or another.

Well, it's now widely believed that Hughes did indeed have OCD. Just to rub salt into the wounds, when I was a little boy, my brother used to call me Howard Hughes for a joke because he said I washed my hands too much. And he was right. After a talk the school headmaster gave us about hygiene, I developed a phobia of germs. I became obsessed with washing my hands properly after I came into contact with anything I deemed risky, which was just about anything at all. As a result I used to get badly chapped hands in the winter and my mum had to put moisturiser on them or they cracked and bled.

When I look back I suppose there were other telltale signs of OCD. I was obsessive about my room and how things were arranged, often having big clear outs and rearranging all the furniture according to top-down drawings I'd done. It felt like there were certain magic combinations which, if achieved, could yield great rewards; but if done wrong, would surely yield bad consequences instead. This visceral kind of intuition has dogged me all my life. It's magical thinking by any other name. Luckily, now I can call it for what it is, and choose to defy it. Well, that's what I like to tell myself anyway(glances nervously over to rabbit's foot, dream catcher and voodoo kettle).

Another possible precursor of OCD was a facial tic I had as a child. The best way of describing such a tic to someone who hasn't had one, is that it feels like you're scratching an otherwise inaccessible itch inside your head. Such tics are more commonly associated with Tourette syndrome. As mentioned previously though, there are strong links between these two disorders, and many people who later go on to develop OCD, remark on having had a facial tic as a child.

As one treacherous journey drew to a close, so another one began. As soon as I realised that my mystery affliction was OCD, I got straight on the phone to the doctor, and booked an appointment to find out what help was available. I was in the driving seat this time.

Interestingly, there was no apology whatsoever from my doctor for missing the correct diagnosis fifteen years earlier. Apparently there's no accountability in that line of work. He's not my doctor any more.

After that I met with a lovely Community Psychiatric Nurse(CPN) who did a thorough Q and A session with me to ascertain whether I really did have OCD. When he was satisfied that I did, he put me on a waiting list for therapy.

From the moment I set foot in the doctor's office, through to my last session of therapy, I was leaned on hard to start taking SSRI medication every single step of the way. I was very reluctant to go down that road again after the bad experience I'd had with SSRI drugs before. Besides, they didn't make a dent in OCD last time, so why should they now? During the hiatus before therapy, I read a great book about OCD - Brain Lock by Dr. Jeffrey M. Schwartz. Somewhere in the book it stated that SSRI drugs weren't strictly necessary when undertaking CBT. So I decided I was going to try it without them. I was taken aback by the resistance that this decision was met with. From the doctor, to the CPN, to the therapists, to welfare workers, I had to defend my decision ad nauseam. But I was determined to stick to my guns come what may.

About five months after seeing the CPN, I was allotted six one-hour sessions of talking therapy. This felt alarmingly brief, but I tried to be positive about it nonetheless. My therapist was a charmless lady who liked to sit staring at me saying nothing for as long as possible. I frequently used to have to prompt her because the clock was ticking and it was her turn to talk. OCD aside, she seemed to have a problem with me as a person - very quick to criticise the answers I gave or the words I used. It all seemed so incredibly unnecessary and inappropriate given the context. Worse than that, she didn't seem to know much about OCD or CBT. I found myself in the embarrassing position of having to plug the gaps with what I'd read in Brain Lock. Then she had the temerity to regurgitate those things back to me in the next session. It was absolutely creepy and surreal. The experience was unexpectedly hostile and unhelpful. I quickly lost all trust in her and terminated the therapy after the fourth session, having learned absolutely nothing.

I felt very dejected after that, like my important revelation had been marginalised and my one shot at getting better had just gone up in smoke. I'd just wasted a lot of time going down yet another dead end.

Everything felt hopeless and I began to feel very alone in my plight. I descended into a strange period of depression after this. I felt hopelessly lost in life and didn't know how to make everything right again. I felt detached from reality and started sleeping for long periods - anything up to sixteen hours at a time. Sleep felt like a sanctuary I could escape to, where I didn't have to think about all the bad things I couldn't face.

Thoughts drifted increasingly towards suicide and I started thinking about how and where I would do it; rehearsing the scenarios over in my head to gauge whether I could actually bring myself to go through with it. The local art gallery had a roof garden which was high enough to do the job. I was considering it as a possibility, so I went to check it out one day. But for the first time in all my visits there, the garden was locked that day. I've never been more relieved and disappointed at the same time. Honestly though, I doubt I would have gone through with it anyway - I'm not very good with heights. I know that probably sounds ridiculous in the circumstances, but still, it is a factor when considering such a thing. Since then, I've intermittently drifted in and out of periods where I've entertained thoughts of suicide.

What I've gleaned from all this is that when I'm low or hopeless or worried, it's easy to flirt with the idea of suicide; to brood on it; even to start thinking practically about how and where I might carry it out. Yet that last step is a big one, and requires either a lot of courage or a lot of despair. I think having easy access to a quick and clean method would make all the difference. I never had that and I always found the available options off-putting in various ways - either too long and drawn out, or not guaranteed to succeed, or traumatising for people to witness. If I'd had access to something that would alleviate those concerns, then I think it may well have tipped the balance.

As it stands, I've never actually started putting the pieces in place to make it happen. I have a hell of a lot of respect for anyone who does though. Well, apart from people who've done wrong and do it to stave off imminent consequences that is. It makes me angry when people roll off trite reprimands about strangers who took their own lives - things like "It's the easy way out" or "How selfish?". I find it vulgar and misplaced. I think these people are missing the point entirely. There's nothing easy about it. It's a terrifying and lonely prospect. When somebody has sunk so desperately low that they're actually considering that as a real possibility, expecting them to carefully rationalise through the consequences of their actions is just too naive.

It was only a good while after my first therapy disappointment, that I realised I could sign up for more than just one lot of therapy. This came as a genuine surprise to me. After more appointments with the doctor and CPN, I was put on a waiting list for therapy once again. After a few months I was allotted twenty one-hour sessions of CBT. Happily, this therapist was the antithesis of the last one. It was a breath of fresh air. She made it clear from the outset that, given my age and the condition I had, there was every chance I couldn't just shake it off with therapy and I may have to live with OCD for the rest of my life. I really appreciated her candour. That's exactly what I needed to hear after all the time I'd wasted being misled.

Nevertheless, she said we could try using CBT to improve things a bit, and maybe provide me with some new ways of dealing with OCD going forward. We eventually tried some ERP therapy to try and reduce the grip of some of my compulsions. Unbeknownst to me I'd already started unwittingly doing some ERP work after reading Brain Lock. The book outlines a very similar process to ERP and I'd started practising it in a fairly disorganised fashion in the months leading up to the therapy. So we built on that, and eventually I made some in-roads in mitigating some of my compulsions.

However, my circumstances at the time did not lend themselves very well to the arduous demands of CBT. I still lived with my parents and didn't get on with my dad. My career up till that point had been a train wreck: a late start, a few bizarre false starts, mis-sold dead end jobs, working in London for a couple of years, redundancy, unable to get another job in London, and finally forced to go back home because I was broke. I'd fallen horribly behind on the ladder. No property, no savings, and a CV by Salvador Dali. I eventually got another job but the pay wasn't great. Worried that rent was just money down the drain, I decided to remain at home, and keep saving until I could afford my own place. So for years, I remained in a job I hated and went without holidays or luxuries. Seven years later, I tried for a mortgage but was refused because I didn't have enough savings and wasn't earning enough. After that, my OCD got so bad that I didn't even entertain the idea of moving out any more; at least not until I felt a good deal better anyway. I was genuinely concerned that I'd end up with a mortgage, but become ill and unemployable, and not be able to keep up the payments. My age was against me now anyway. Then I lost my job and everything fell to pieces. All bets were off. Relations had steadily worsened between me and my dad over the years, so it was like walking on eggshells at home. I was trapped in an absolute living nightmare.

Some new neighbours moved in on the side adjacent to my bedroom window, and they had a lot of building work done. I'm particularly noise sensitive and too many interruptions invariably exacerbate my OCD. When that eventually died down, a large building site was promptly set up directly behind our house, which meant there was loud mechanised whirring and banging six days a week for the next year.

In the midst of all this, my car developed a nightmarish problem that no one seemed capable of diagnosing. Unable to just give up driving or pay the outrageous dealership prices, I was forced to become an amateur mechanic for a year, while I pin-pointed and fixed the problem. Suffice to say, the experience kicked my OCD into overdrive.

With my parents getting older, I found myself having to take on more and more responsibilities at home - as a chauffeur, a cleaner, a dishwasher, a shopper, an odd job man, a gardener, an errand boy. Some of these duties played havoc with my OCD. Trying to deal with rampant pure O while driving people around or pushing a trolley around a supermarket is no kind of fun. Not to mention the multiple ironies of somebody with OCD having to clean a hoarder's house, while said hoarder stands smugly criticising how they're going about it(*see Hoovering the Hoarder's House*).

I watched in horror as my time was being divided up between these duties and my therapy commitments. All the while, my already-depleted savings were dwindling further and further. I lamented all of those tough years at work, putting myself through a daily OCD hell, thinking it would get me to a point where I could finally afford my own place. Somewhere along the road I'd stumbled, and now I was pinned down under heavy fire, watching it all slip through my fingers at a horrifying rate. It felt unforgivable and I hated myself for it.

Nevertheless, I'd been re-assured in therapy that there was nothing to worry about, because that's what benefits were there for. Apparently once my savings dipped below a certain limit, there was a safety net to cushion the blow. Well, when my savings did fall below that limit, a year-long nightmarish ordeal commenced as the welfare services subjected me to their deeply unpleasant and violating claims process. I had no concept of what awaited me there. I was like a lamb to the slaughter.

I'd been blown away by the gains I started making with ERP, especially in the absence of the sacred medication. And make no mistake, they were hard-won gains - very much a case of "two steps forward, one step back". Given enough time, therapy and financial support, who knows what I might have been able to accomplish? Back in the real world though, with the wolves at the door and these combined pressures bearing down on me from all sides, it soon became apparent that the gains I'd previously made, were being washed away like so many sand castles at high tide. In the meantime the therapy came to an abrupt end and I was left in no man's land.

In hindsight, I concluded that certain prerequisites really need to be in place before someone can realistically be expected to undertake that kind of work. Within reason, financial pressures and circumstances promoting anxiety need to be removed. Without that foundation, it's just a cruel waste of time.

Sometimes insufficient help can be more of a hindrance than nothing at all. It doesn't actually fix the problem it's supposed to be fixing. It burns up precious time and money which you could have used more pragmatically to tackle cold hard priorities in life instead. That in turn would have created a better climate for addressing your original problem going forward. The truth that you will never hear out there on the forums and in the press, is that the calibre of support really required to help people with soul-crushing conditions like OCD, is simply not there. Ultimately, you are on your own. You either have enough time and money to throw at the problem, or it's up to you to somehow navigate the contradictions, and figure your way out of the impossible mess you're in. Sure, you can learn some useful techniques from books or from your allotted ration of CBT, but you have to go away and do the work yourself. You have to be your own physician. And that is extremely difficult to do in the face of financial pressures and stressful circumstances at home. There is nothing worse than winning the fight of your life, only to find that dark forces stole away your victory in the night while you slept.

In the absence of the kind of support I really needed, I realised that I'd just have to forget about therapy for the time being, and shoulder my OCD the best I could until I somehow addressed my financial problems myself. Of course, it goes without saying that in an ideal world, the OCD should have been my number one priority, but it was completely out of my hands. Therapy was an unachievable time and money drain that I could no longer responsibly entertain in the face of a precarious looking future.

And that pretty much brings us up to the present day. I'm grateful for the therapy I received and proud of the improvements I made. I'm especially proud that I made those improvements without taking any SSRI medication. Seriously, if I can do that under those difficult circumstances, then I think there's hope for anyone. Wherever I can, I try to use what I learned to eschew my compulsions and not let any new obsessions creep in. What can I tell you though - it's always at odds with everything else going on around me these days. OCD feeds off stress and worry and I've been immersed in it since I finished work. The way I look at it now, OCD is like a test I have to sit each day. The human mind is in constant flux. There are good days and there are bad days.

On the good days, I find there are less triggers and they're easier to resist. I love those days. I feel like a normal human being again. On the bad days, there are more triggers and they're harder to get a handle on. On those days, it feels like OCD was waiting impatiently while I slept. It leaps onto my back as soon as I wake up, and rides me until my mind grinds to an aching halt. It's a very defeating sensation, feeling so ill and exhausted just after you've woken up. Those days, it can get out of control, like a game of Whack-a-Mole that keeps growing in size and increasing in speed. When it gets away from me, I have to kid myself that I can do some kind of one-size-fits-all exorcism on all the left-over odd socks tumbling around in my head. But deep down, I know that it's breaking all of the rules, that it's a cop out, and I hate myself for doing it. Deep down, I know there's a huge outstanding debt accruing in some parallel dimension; all the ones I let through into the net; all the ones that got away. And that will never sit right.

Somehow I suspect this unwelcome stowaway will remain on board until the end of my voyage, but I'll keep working on it whenever and however I can. After all, it's the only game in town so what the hell have I got to lose! In the meantime, all I can afford to do is live with it best I can, while I tread water with my obligations, and try to find a way out of the horrible mess that I'm in. It's not the kind of happy ending we're accustomed to reading about whenever mental health problems are discussed in the media. Nevertheless, it's where I'm really at with this thing, and I don't know how to tell it to you any other way.

It's certainly not my intention to paint a bleak picture without hope here. However I absolutely refuse to bullshit people to fulfil an agenda or sell more books. Both in my life and in my journey with OCD, I've found false hope to be more damaging than an absence of hope. False hope seduces us down toxic blind alleyways, when instead we should be facing up to cold hard realities and taking the necessary action to change things for the better. Besides, I believe there is still plenty of hope to be had here. There is hope of spreading OCD awareness through books like this. In turn, there is hope people will discover they have OCD when they're aged twelve instead of forty-two. There is hope of discovering that you're not alone; that you're not a freak; that your private nightmare is actually a well-documented problem which many other people are also going through. There is hope of learning how it works and finding new ways to deal with it, so that you don't always have to respond "How high?" whenever it comes shouting "Jump!". There is hope of finding a way to live with this thing in a state of realistic acceptance rather than in a state of civil war or denial. I hope that is a place that we as sufferers can all get to.

Appendix 3 - About Depression

I will keep this appendix fairly brief because I feel like public awareness about depression is significantly better than it is about OCD, so there's a lot less room for misconceptions. As such, I'll just cover the absolute basics, and talk a little about my experience.

Depression is a common mental health condition, whereby a person loses all hope and feels inconsolably low for prolonged periods of time. They no longer derive pleasure from the things or people they used to. The joy gradually drains away from their lives, and everything feels pointless or harder than it ought to be. Irritability and feelings of worthlessness likely follow. They're inclined to withdraw into their shell as a result. A self-reinforcing positive feedback loop is set up, driven by despair and isolation. Their outlook inevitably deteriorates as a result. Sufferers often report feeling numb or trapped behind a wall of glass.

Depression varies in severity. When it's mild, it may not impact on one's quality of life too much and may even cease altogether over time without any external intervention. When it's severe though, it will impact dramatically upon one's quality of life, and is likely to result in suicidal ideation or even suicide. Depressed people tend to cry more often than usual, sometimes without any apparent stimulus. Depression has an adverse effect on eating and sleeping patterns, either leading to excesses or deprivations. It's very common for depressed people to self-medicate with alcohol or other drugs. In theory, doing physical exercise can temporarily lift your mood when you're depressed. In reality though, it tends to be about the last thing you feel like doing when you're "down with the black dog". Depression is usually treated with psychotherapy, but anti-depressant medication may also be prescribed in more severe cases.

I first experienced symptoms of depression when I was about thirteen. I found myself wrestling some bleak new feelings I didn't understand and didn't know what to do with. I felt increasingly estranged from my peers and inexplicably hopeless about life. I would sometimes get home from school and cry for no discernible reason. I found myself inclined to go for walks on my own and involuntarily gravitated towards the melancholy. Without wishing to sound pretentious, I think depression just became a way of life for me after that. Now, I don't even know where depression ends and where I begin. I don't know what I would look like without it.

When you're depressed, positivity is an elusive and precious commodity. Left to your own devices you will likely be stuck moving in ever decreasing circles in a world devoid of hope or positivity. In the throes of depression, I find it difficult to conjure up a positive mood, and maintain it for any useful length of time. It feels like clawing my way up a treacherous ice-clad rock face and making camp; only to awaken the next morning and find that I slid all the way back down again during the night. Some of my poems reflect this.

To that end, I used to indulge in desperate escapism when I was younger. While at secondary school, I was deeply disturbed by the tawdry day-to-day drudgery I found myself trapped in. Increasingly alienated, I felt very strongly that I didn't belong in that world, and I struggled to cope with it. Whenever I stumbled on something that felt more like me - music, cinema, buildings, places, styles, ideas - I would automatically become a collector of paraphernalia about that thing. Not real objects you understand, but ideas which I would gradually gather and assemble into a collage inside my mind. A secret fantasy world I could project on top of the real one, and lose myself inside(*see Bubble Wrap*). It's a horribly flawed and fragile existence, but nonetheless, it got me through some tough times at school. In retrospect, I spent many years in a state of deluded self-hypnosis to endure what felt utterly unendurable to me at the time. If I'm honest with myself, I never really stopped doing this, but I think it's fair to say that I learned to do it with one foot planted on the ground. It's hard to pull off when you're extremely down though. Self-motivation is a real problem in such circumstances. Sometimes, treading water is the best you can hope for.

I think it's fair to say that I've found depression easier to dance with as I've grown older, but I'm also aware that this could change at any point. In my case, I have to say that OCD has been the source of much more pain and difficulty than depression has. However, I do acknowledge that some people experience a kind of relentless all-consuming depression, the likes of which I've never known. It brings otherwise capable people to their knees and its devastating effects should never be underestimated. I sometimes wonder if a desperate upside of OCD might be that it pushes the depression into the background by stealing so much time, energy and focus.

That's all I'm inclined to say about depression for the purposes of this book, but there are many recommended books available on the subject should you wish to find out more.

301

Appendix 4 - Drinking the Kool-aid

A fabled old African proverb says "A speaker of truth has no friends". What the saying neglects to mention however, is that loathsome misguided buffoons have no friends either. In other words, you're not automatically right just because you're going against the grain.

To assume such a thing would be an example of a *false dichotomy* - i.e. stating that something must be either A or B, with no in-between, when in reality it's not a black and white issue at all. Such devices are frequently used in politics, religion, and advertising; usually when someone wants to ram something down your throat which you might otherwise have trouble swallowing.

The purpose of this section is to try and explain why I've expressed certain controversial opinions in some of my poems. I'm telling you what I think, and why I think it. I'm not telling you what you should think. Once again, I feel obliged to remind the reader that I'm not qualified in medicine, psychotherapy, pharmacology. So I'm in no position to advise anyone else on these things, and it's not my wish to do so. If you're troubled by any of the issues I raise here, then I'd strongly urge you to put down this book, and seek out some recommended books written by qualified experts instead. I felt it important to preface this section with these points, as I'm going to go against the grain on some controversial issues here. And as we know, that does not necessarily make me right.

Here I'm going to talk about the pharmaceutical drugs and therapy used to treat OCD. According to the UK's National Institute for Health and Care Excellence(NICE), the recommended treatment for OCD is a combination of Cognitive Behavioural Therapy(CBT) and Selective Serotonin Reuptake Inhibitor(SSRI) medication.

In simplest terms, CBT is used to analyse people's negative responses to certain things, and work on ways of improving those responses. CBT is a broad field and can be used in various ways to treat a whole range of mental disorders. When treating OCD, it tends to take the form of Exposure Response Prevention(ERP) therapy, which is aimed at gradually weaning OCD sufferers off their compulsions through will power alone. Sometimes other incarnations of CBT are used to treat OCD - such as Acceptance and Commitment

Therapy(ACT) - but ERP is the most widely used approach here in the UK.

SSRI medication is the most commonly prescribed form of anti-depressant in many countries throughout the world. It increases the amount of *serotonin* in play in the brain, by blocking receptors which would otherwise take it back out of circulation. Serotonin is a naturally occurring chemical in the human brain, which is widely thought to have an influence on happiness and well-being. So these pills are supposed to make people calmer and happier by increasing the active amount of serotonin in their brains.

I am not against pharmaceutical drugs or therapy per se. Evidently some OCD sufferers are helped by CBT and SSRI medication. Some even claim to be completely cured by the combination. I made some temporary progress in mitigating my own compulsions using CBT therapy. Under the right circumstances, I believe that CBT can be effective in reducing current compulsions, and possibly limiting future entanglements as well.

What I'm about to discuss here isn't whether CBT and SSRI medication *can* be effective. It's about the bold claims that get cooked up about these things by all the wrong people for all the wrong reasons. It's about how those claims end up being weaponised against OCD sufferers. More importantly it's about the damaging position this can leave OCD sufferers in.

I've found that certain tacit assumptions get made about OCD by government welfare services, by the medical establishment, and sometimes even by OCD charities:

- One is that OCD is a homogeneous entity that anyone can catch and lose, much like a cold.

- Another one is that anyone diagnosed with OCD should immediately be put on SSRI medication for the foreseeable future.

- Yet another is that CBT and SSRI medication are a neat cure for OCD. If the cure doesn't work, then the only possible explanation is that the sufferer wasn't medicated enough or wasn't trying hard enough, in that order.

- The crowning assumption is that anyone who disagrees with these assumptions has a bad attitude and doesn't really want to get better. Therefore they lose the right to be taken seriously from that point onwards.

These assumptions are projected onto OCD sufferers throughout their dealings with doctors, therapists and welfare services - all the key players in their diagnosis and post-diagnosis journey. By invisible capillary action, these ideas gradually permeate wider society and influence the opinions of family, friends and employers; who latch onto them and casually wield them as facts in conversations with sufferers.

OCD is still very much a nascent disorder. Given how our understanding has evolved regarding similar abstruse phenomena throughout human history, I think it's safe to assume that our view of OCD is likely to be somewhat different in fifty years time to what it is now. Yet these key players would have us believe that they already know everything there is to know about OCD right now. These assumptions beg the question, but apparently we're expected to just fall in line and blindly accept them without rocking the boat. Indeed, if you are impertinent enough to question them, you risk being ridiculed, intimidated, ostracised or financially penalised.

So whom do these assumptions serve exactly?

Perhaps the OCD sufferer?

Well, not if they're strong-armed into taking medication they'd rather not take, and experience some of the less publicised side effects, such as lucid nightmares, swollen tongues, dry mouths, the inability to cry, diminished sexual libido, or suicidal ideation. What if the sufferer is against taking medication for perfectly valid reasons? Maybe they had a bad experience with it in the past; or they're not convinced that these substances and their wider effects are truly understood by the people doling them out; or they're taking a moral stand against questionable practices engaged in by the pharmaceutical industry. Why is their opinion so readily dismissed or ridiculed?

And what about the many OCD sufferers who earnestly undertake CBT but are left uncured? What about the resulting implication that they didn't try hard enough or weren't medicated enough? There's every chance they'll end up unemployed because of their condition. So where does this perceived failure leave them with the welfare services who regard CBT and medication as a neat cure for OCD? Do they conclude that the sufferer simply couldn't be bothered getting better?

Do they misinterpret the sufferer's choice not to take medication as a lack of commitment? Do they infer that the sufferer's attitude or honesty are in question? In turn, how does this impact on the sufferer's eligibility for unemployment and sickness benefits, which they should be entitled to with a diagnosis of OCD?

So if these assumptions don't serve the OCD sufferer, then whom do they serve?

Perhaps the government who happily brandish this false dichotomy of "cured or invalid" to massage statistics so that there are less mouths to feed? Perhaps pharmaceutical companies who profit from the vast amounts of medication prescribed? Perhaps private healthcare companies who have a constant queue of OCD recidivists waiting to go back through the revolving doors for therapy?

Well, I do question these assumptions. I find them flawed, downright offensive, and damaging to OCD sufferers. I suspect they're no more than convenient devices conceived by private industry in collusion with capitalist governments; allowing the former to generate colossal amounts of revenue, and the latter to wriggle out of their rightful responsibility towards those with crushing mental health problems. In the meantime, the neglected burden of responsibility is shifted squarely onto the shoulders of OCD sufferers, who are in effect blamed for not taking advantage of the magic cure; blamed for having a bad attitude; blamed for having OCD.

At the mercy of a society drunk on these assumptions, an OCD sufferer can either embrace the therapy/medication and agree that they're cured at the end of it, or apostatise and agree that they don't have OCD after all, or else be labelled a fraud and face trial by ordeal with the welfare services.

Despite the attempted whitewash, I think there are still plenty of grey areas worthy of discussion, and many valid questions which still need asking, such as:

- Could OCD be the product of a genetically inherited brain defect, rather than something which is learned or caught? Perhaps it could even be all three of these things, or something else entirely?

- Is it possible that OCD is not a homogeneous entity after all, and there's some variation between different people? Perhaps it's even more than one disorder piled into the same bucket?

- Can a corporately sponsored government really be entrusted with setting the parameters for what OCD is, and what constitutes a cure? Surely such a government will always be inclined to minimise unemployment figures, cut back on welfare costs, and champion the interests of its lobbyists and benefactors, rather than those of the sick and the poor.

- Is it possible that CBT and SSRI medication are not effective on some OCD sufferers, no matter how hard they try?

- Is CBT just a cosmetic exercise which, best case scenario, clears up a sufferer's current compulsions, but leaves OCD's underlying driving mechanism untouched?

- If CBT is indeed just a cosmetic exercise, then whom does it serve to label sufferers as "cured" once treatment ends?

- When interfacing with welfare and mental health services, why are OCD sufferers always subjected to the overarching assumption that they should be taking SSRI medication? Why is it that only medicated people are taken seriously? Why is the consumption of prescription drugs regarded as a touchstone of whether a person really has OCD, or whether they're serious about therapy?

- Why can't CBT be attempted without medication first?

- Why are doctors and therapists so cavalier about the side effects of SSRIs? They affect people in different ways and there are a lot of unknown quantities here; not least of all, reports of elevated suicide rates among people taking them.

- Is it possible that SSRI medication merely masks the real problems behind OCD and depression? Could it be giving people the illusion that they're better, when in reality nothing fundamental has changed, and they're just drunk on serotonin? What happens when the medication finally stops, and new stressors are introduced into their lives?

The part of this that troubles me most is the ubiquitous coercion to take medication throughout the OCD sufferer's post-diagnosis journey. Like I said before, I am not against pharmaceutical products per se. I'm aware that they're the best available treatment for disorders involving psychosis. I also accept that they're worth trying when people are brought to their knees by things like OCD and depression. Furthermore I think they're an absolute godsend for people suffering from painful, life-threatening or crippling conditions like cancer, arthritis or epilepsy. I've taken them myself for a number of ailments. I am not a pharmaceutical Luddite by any means.

I just question whether we should so readily acquiesce to regarding pharmaceuticals as a panacea for all of our health problems. This way of thinking seems to be woven into the very fabric of our society now. I worry that we're all being insidiously weaned on the teat of lifelong pharmaceutical dependency.

More specifically, I question whether SSRI drugs should always be prescribed for OCD and depression. Perhaps medication should be a last resort, only to be considered if therapy proves impossible without it. Perhaps it would be more empowering for people to first try and locate the root causes of their problems, and find a way of overcoming them without the chemical crutch.

On an ethical level, I question whether the responsibility for researching and developing these drugs should be put in the hands of corporations, whose sole driving force is to make as much profit as possible for their shareholders. Therein lies the problem. These corporations have been allowed to occupy a privileged position which is surely only fit for objective altruists untainted by the lures of profit and competition. A position which should be reserved for scientists with a mandate to find the best possible solutions, which are then made available to the patient at the lowest possible cost.

Of course, I appreciate how laughably naive that last part must sound through the lens of a modern capitalist plutocracy. But perhaps the cynicism with which we greet such ideas, is a sad reflection of how far we've fallen from grace; of how readily we endorse practices which are inherently detrimental to the most vulnerable people in our society; the very people who need healthcare the most: the sick and the poor.

Pharmaceutical companies' profit margins alone tell us how good a deal we're getting from them. Thanks to these staggering profits, they've been able to remodel the playing field unrecognisably in their favour; to the point where they now have an extremely unhealthy and unwarranted influence over our governments and healthcare systems.

We hear the most disturbing reports of pharmaceutical companies indulging in questionable practices like:

- repurposing off-patent drugs for conditions they weren't even developed or trialled for. They do this to recoup the cost of trials and development, when they deem that not enough people have the condition to make developing a bespoke drug for it sufficiently profitable.

- paying family doctors commission to push their drugs for certain conditions.

- deliberately pricing crucial drugs(like cancer drugs) so outrageously high, that the UK's National Health Service(NHS) can't afford them; while simultaneously funding the very charities who pressure the NHS into using those drugs, in spite of their inflated price tags.

- similar to the previous scenario: deliberately pricing vital drugs so astronomically high that people who need them are forced to beg charities for financial aid. The drug company funds those same charities to exploit a loophole whereby the government then has to reimburse the drug company with much more money than they originally funded - i.e. a pre-meditated long con to steal money out of the public purse, apparently with the government's blessing.

- funding political lobbyists and supposedly impartial healthcare decision makers - e.g. political parties, experts on drug regulating boards, experts on panels deciding which drugs are used by the NHS, and experts who recommend strategies for managing the NHS going forward.

With all of this happening right under our noses, can we really afford to be so naive as to blindly trust these companies and their products?

In 1940s Great Britain, the creation of the NHS represented the pinnacle of healthcare reforms which had been hard fought for since Victorian times. It made basic healthcare a human right for all citizens, rather than a luxury only available to the wealthy. We are now on the cusp of witnessing its destruction by the super rich who clearly don't need it themselves, and cynically regard it as a slice of the pie they're not getting a taste of.

Pharmaceutical and private healthcare companies stand to make an absolute killing(no pun intended) on the back of the NHS's downfall.

As such, they're doing everything in their power to undermine and destroy it. Apparently our elected representatives in Westminster are only too happy to stand aside and take funding from them while they do it. This in turn means our leaders are beholden to those companies when it comes to making decisions about the NHS going forward. This has been reflected by decades of funding cuts, hospital closures, constantly moved goalposts, and the NHS being increasingly forced to contract out its services to private healthcare companies; companies which often use clever offshore accounting tricks to wriggle out of paying any UK tax. The government has not only failed miserably to protect the NHS on behalf of the British people, but it has effectively held the back door wide open and allowed private healthcare to quietly creep in unchecked. Clearly something's gone fundamentally wrong here and the infected tail is wagging the dog to death.

Then we come to the issue of overmedication - i.e. pharmaceutical drugs being marketed beyond their legitimate remit purely for profit. Within a capitalist economy, it goes without saying that companies will always be looking to expand their customer base. If we conveniently ignore issues like over-consumption, then maybe this is harmless enough when it results in, say, people buying a garden gnome when they don't really need one. However, alarm bells start ringing when this practice strays into sacrosanct territory affecting our health and well being; like pharmaceutical medication for instance.

To understand how such a situation could come to pass, we have to look at the evolution of psychiatry over the last 40 years. In the US, psychiatry began to lose its credibility in the 1960s and 1970s. It was criticised for engendering too many conflicting schools of thought and lacking common standards. Its nuanced diagnoses were deemed too ambiguous to yield efficient results. It was becoming marginalised as an inconsistent pseudoscience that didn't treat real diseases. As a result, psychiatrists were finding it increasingly difficult to get academic funding and reimbursement from medical insurance companies.

An embattled US psychiatric establishment decided that it needed to make psychiatry look more like a scientific discipline to silence the critics. To this end, it partnered with the pharmaceutical industry in the early 1980s to champion a new psychopharmacological approach to mental healthcare in the US. Their secret weapon in all this was the Diagnostic and Statistical Manual of Mental Disorders(DSM) produced by the American Psychiatric Association(ACA) - the psychiatric bible in the US.

To a certain extent, the wheels had already been set in motion when the previous edition of the DSM stopped referring to mental health problems as "reactions". This subtly shifted the burden of causality away from environmental factors and onto the individual. Furthermore, psychiatrists had already started using psychotropic drugs alongside therapy to treat certain disorders.

However, a complete paradigm shift occurred in 1980, when the DSM was updated to its third iteration: DSM-III. This repackaged existing mental health disorders and created many brand new ones out of thin air. These disorders were pigeon-holed into discrete self-contained categories. Each disorder was defined by a list of behaviours picked from a shared standardised list. These behaviours could be ticked off against a given patient's symptoms to form an expeditious diagnosis. Some of these behaviours had previously been regarded as normal behaviours, or at least not attributable to mental illness - e.g. sadness, grief, shyness, stress, boredom or anti-authoritarianism. Among the new and repackaged disorders were depression, generalised anxiety disorder, social phobia, post traumatic stress disorder, attention deficit disorder, autism, bipolar disorder, and obsessive compulsive disorder.

Whether by accident or design, the growing implication was that people with mental health problems had something biologically wrong with them which needed fixing. And apparently the way to fix it was by taking daily pharmaceutical medication. So while the ACA got busy providing psychiatrists with a paint-by-numbers approach to diagnosis in the form of the DSM-III, pharmaceutical companies got busy matching their drugs up to the disorders listed within it.

In the US, pharmaceutical advertising and mental health awareness campaigns were rolled out across the media. The outcome was a goldrush for big pharma, psychiatry, private healthcare and health insurance companies; all of whom cashed in on the resulting stampede. The government didn't complain because it was all good business and the implied burden of responsibility had been subtly shifted from the state onto individuals.

Now it's important to note that the DSM's usage was confined to the US. The UK and the rest of the world favoured a manual produced by the World Health Organisation(WHO), called the International

Classification of Diseases(ICD). When the DSM-III was released, these two manuals were still substantially different. However the DSM's structure increasingly influenced the ICD going forward. In part, this was due to deliberate collaboration between the ACA and the WHO with a view to aligning their categorisations more closely. It was also fuelled by ongoing efforts by the ACA to market the DSM outside the US to boost the revenue it received from its sale. More importantly though, many psychiatrists working on the DSM and the ICD had ties to the pharmaceutical industry, whose interests were better served by the DSM's new approach. This combination of factors meant that the rest of the world fell in line with the new US psychopharmacological model soon enough; markedly so with the advent of the ICD 10(1992) and the DSM-IV(1994). As with so many things, the goldrush subsequently spread throughout the UK and Europe, lagging slightly behind the US.

The pharmaceutical advertising used in the US was prohibited in the UK though. So instead, pharmaceutical companies concentrated their efforts on the multimedia awareness campaigns which had been so effective in the US. These campaigns were designed to make people wonder whether they had a disorder by listing the kind of symptoms to look out for, and by getting people with the disorder to open up and share their story. If it was suddenly acceptable to talk about these hitherto taboo subjects on national TV, then maybe it was OK for people to go and discuss such problems with their family doctor.

On paper, this all seemed like a positive change. Genuine sufferers, previously oblivious of their conditions were being edified, diagnosed and helped instead of suffering in silence. Surely it was a win-win situation for everyone? However, the glossy media veneer concealed some ugly cracks.

First of all, the media awareness campaigns deliberately cast a very wide net, using those newly pathologised normal behaviours set out in the DSM/ICD as examples of symptoms to look out for. Inevitably people ended up wrongly diagnosed or self-diagnosed. Even those correctly diagnosed were led to believe that the available treatment was more effective than it really was, and the side effects were played down. Sometimes drugs not only failed to help with the diagnosed disorder, but spawned unexpected secondary disorders, e.g. bipolar disorder in the case of depression and ADHD.

Secondly, the very cornerstone upon which this psychopharmacological doctrine was built - the DSM-III - had some inherent flaws:

- its categorisations and criteria were driven by expert opinion rather than empirical scientific evidence

- it conveniently eschewed the nuanced nature of mental health problems in favour of crowd-pleasing pigeon holing and apparent quick fixes

- it failed to consider external stressors as possible causes for mental health problems

- many of the new criteria used to define disorders had previously been regarded as normal behaviours

- a substantial amount of its authors had ties with pharmaceutical companies, raising questions about conflict of interest

- its new *descriptive* approach of ticking symptoms off against a checklist, appeared scientific on the face of it. In reality though, it could too easily mistake normal human traits as grounds for a diagnosis

In fairness, the authors of the DSM-III did warn that the manual was not strictly supported by empirical data. As such, they urged psychotherapists not to rely on it exclusively when making diagnoses. Nevertheless, the ease of diagnosis and profitability offered by the DSM-III made it appealing to psychiatrists and pharmaceutical companies alike. So they inevitably gravitated towards its usage contrary to the warnings. The chairman of the task force who created the DSM-III, Robert Spitzer, was later quoted as saying it led to the medicalisation of 20-30% of the population who may not have had any serious mental problems.

Thirdly, we come to SSRI drugs - one of the mainstays of the pharmaceutical arsenal wielded to serve this new model. When they first came on the scene in the early 1990s, SSRIs were promoted as the drug of choice for treating depression and anxiety disorders - a trend which has continued to this day. The link between depression and low serotonin levels was heavily touted by psychiatrists and doctors to push the perception of SSRIs as a cure for depression. People were sold the idea of needing daily medication to correct a "chemical imbalance" in their brains - an easy off-the-shelf fix for a simple biological defect. Both of these ideas have since been increasingly scrutinised, even within the psychiatric establishment, and they're beginning to look remarkably dubious at this point. Yet people are still freely talking in these terms to prop up this profitable model.

Despite these alarming failings, this psychopharmacological approach to mental healthcare was wholeheartedly embraced by Western governments. The resulting goldrush is still in full swing today. In the decades since the DSM-III's release, vast numbers of adults have voluntarily presented themselves at doctors' surgeries to be casually diagnosed and prescribed pharmaceutical drugs which they may well have ended up taking for the rest of their lives. Once the adult market was saturated, children became the new market, focussing on disorders like autism, bipolar, depression and ADHD. Apparently now they're trying to convince us that our babies and pets need medicating too.

These are dark times indeed for the human race. The collusion between governments and private companies regarding mental healthcare brings to mind a prediction Aldous Huxley made in an interview with Mike Wallace in 1958:

"[If you want to preserve your power indefinitely, you have to get the consent of the ruled. And this they will do, partly by drugs as I foresaw in Brave New World, partly by these new techniques of propaganda. They will do it by bypassing the sort of rational side of man, and appealing to his subconscious and his deeper emotions, and his physiology even. And so making him actually love his slavery. I mean, I think this is the danger: that actually people may be in some ways happy under the new regime, but they will be happy in situations where they oughtn't to be happy.]"

I think that last part is particularly pertinent. I worry that we are being sedated into ignoring problems which shouldn't be ignored, both in society and in ourselves. I suspect that perfectly natural human reactions to the more dehumanising aspects of modern society are being misrepresented as biological flaws in people. Meanwhile society is conveniently let off the hook, while people are forced to correct the perceived flaw with medication and therapy. If that doesn't work, then they're blamed and penalised.

This makes us pitifully controllable and surrenders a lot of power up to our governments. It's a means of subduing dissent down to manageable levels, while repackaging the remainder as mental illness. It makes it all too easy for those in power to impose upon us a cookie-cutter idea of what they think a human being should be. But is any of it for the greater good? Or is it simply to divert money and power into the hands of a few people at the expense of the rest?

I think it's high time the common man woke up and realised that pharmaceutical companies and private healthcare companies are not our friends. Yet they've managed to wrestle a terrifying grip over our governments and healthcare systems. We need to be hyper-vigilant when it comes to the interplay between these companies and our governments, as the potential for corruption has already been demonstrated beyond any doubt, and there's simply too much at stake to just ignore the problem and hope it goes away.

I think sufferers and non-sufferers alike should think twice before blindly deciding to ingest potent chemical cocktails on a daily basis. We used to put this decision in the hands of our trusted family doctor, but can we still trust their judgement when they could well be on the payroll of a pharmaceutical company? Besides, do doctors and psychotherapists truly understand the effects of taking these pills, beyond an entry in a textbook which they may or may not have read? Or are they just parroting whatever the pharmaceutical company sales rep' told them to say, and saying it boldly enough that we don't dare question it any further?

Like I said at the outset, I am not against pharmaceutical products per se. In the right hands, I think they are both necessary and useful when treating a wide range of health problems. I am simply against the way they've been nefariously misappropriated by private interests and manipulated against the common man in pursuit of obscene profit and unwarranted power. As somebody whose life has been dogged by mental illness, I particularly resent the collusion between these private interests and my government to cynically exploit my problem while purporting to care about it.

By the same token, I'm not against talking therapy per se. It can help people with a range of mental health problems. Under the right circumstances, CBT can help some OCD sufferers mitigate their current compulsions. I made some temporary progress with my compulsions through CBT. However, I do believe that therapists and non-sufferers often underestimate what a difficult and violating experience ERP is(ERP is the branch of CBT usually used to treat OCD). Because when you get down to it, all it really amounts to is "Yeah, so just stop doing your compulsions, and tolerate the intolerable anxiety while the problem slowly erodes away". I can attest that this is an incredibly torturous thing to attempt in the face of life's day-to-day demands and pressures. Especially in the absence of any financial support, slowly watching your life savings trickle away, while a therapist glibly tells you that none of that matters, and you should just focus on the therapy. Well that's easy for them to say!

There's something else that ERP glosses over as well. There's a very good reason why people with OCD resort to these strange rituals when exposed to overwhelming fears and doubts which they don't have a conventional answer for. The rituals are intuitively developed as a last-ditch purifying rite that feels absolutely necessary to prevent damage on a spiritual level. That's why they're called compulsions. One feels compelled by a higher power to perform the ritual or else terrible consequences surely await. And it doesn't even matter how deluded that belief is, or how unreal those consequences may be in everyone else's eyes. The feeling that the sufferer is left with when they don't perform the ritual is very real indeed, and believe me when I tell you it feels like nothing on earth.

Now if the ERP process was reasonably brief and got rid of OCD for good, then I could see a strong argument for being cruel to be kind; for pushing sufferers to soldier on through the pain and violation come what may; even for encouraging sufferers to temporarily take medication if it enabled the otherwise impossible completion of the process.

However, based on conversations with many fellow sufferers and from my own experience, I have grave doubts whether this process is as effective as prevailing wisdom would have us believe it is. I wonder how many people are being dosed up and put through a violating nightmare again and again, only for their compulsions to return once therapy ends and the medication is taken away. Because frankly, that is unacceptable. The beleaguered OCD sufferer has to walk away with their tail between their legs and live with the utterly disgusting implication that they've somehow failed to embrace an available cure. No one puts it quite in those terms, but it is very much implied whenever dealing with welfare services, and sometimes even doctors and OCD charity staff. This is a counter-productive, barbaric way to treat people who have already spent much of their lives battling demons the likes of which most people can't even imagine. These people do not need to be subjected to any more cruel humiliating mind games. They do not need to be blamed for any more things which are not their fault. But that is precisely what the welfare services do as a matter of course.

Some people claim that a few sessions of CBT cured their OCD completely. Their success stories get recycled repeatedly on OCD forums and in feelgood magazine articles. In the meantime, the bar gets set higher for uncured sufferers who are made to feel like failures for not matching their success. Without wishing to offend those people, I have to wonder whether they either have some kind of superficial form of OCD, or they've simply been misdiagnosed. In some other cases where OCD is more substantial, sometimes sustained CBT appears to be successful. This is usually accompanied by a prescription of SSRI drugs which are continued indefinitely after treatment ends. I do wonder though if it's merely ridding sufferers of their latest compulsions, while leaving OCD's underlying driving mechanism untouched. A bit like clearing the cobwebs out of the pantry, but leaving the spiders behind, lurking in the cracks, waiting to re-emerge and spin more webs once the door's closed. I'd be interested to know how many people who are said to be cured by CBT this way, later go on to develop further obsessions and compulsions once their SSRI medication is stopped and they're exposed to intolerable circumstances again. Or perhaps as sufferers, we're all meant to acquiesce to being medicated on SSRI drugs for the rest of our lives? Well, that's not an acceptable solution for me I'm afraid, and it's certainly not the way that medication is proposed to sufferers at the outset. It was always meant to be a temporary proposition.

At the very least, I have to question whether CBT should be regarded as a sure-fire cure for all OCD sufferers. It's been demonstrated to me beyond any reasonable doubt that this simply is not the case. And no matter how anyone dresses it up, that is very much how it's regarded out there currently by welfare services. Even some OCD charities talk in these terms and are very quick to censure anyone on their support forums who doesn't toe the line. I wonder if they embrace this neat solution to a difficult problem, in part to make their support role easier, but also to justify their existence. Thus simplifying their role down to a sign-posting function - parroting some textbook spiel and pointing people towards a freely available cure. But then if the cure doesn't work, the blame resides squarely with the sufferer for not being medicated enough or for not trying hard enough, and all they can do is keep going back through the revolving doors. I know that there is a lot of genuine good intention on the part of charity employees, but I fear that they may be unwittingly perpetuating a mythology they don't understand to justify their funding and keep people in jobs.

The assumptions I outlined at the beginning of this section are destroying vulnerable people's lives by depriving them of the crucial support they need when they're at their lowest point. This is reflected by the glut of suicides among people with mental health conditions like OCD in recent years. Successive governments have made draconian changes to the benefits assessment process, taking full advantage of these assumptions to invalidate legitimate claims. The victims of these suicides were either flat refused benefits, or had already been through the violating assessment process before, and just couldn't face the trauma again.

From a subjective point of view, my experience as an OCD sufferer interfacing with the welfare services in the UK was one of the most sinister ordeals I've been subjected to in my entire life. This shocked me because it was the opposite of what I expected, given the nature of my condition, and the service which they purport to provide. I foolishly thought that having such a condition would make that process a foregone conclusion, or at least that I'd be treated with some degree of respect because of my diagnosis. Yet somehow it seems to go the other way with these people. There's a deeply misplaced air of contempt at work there which is hard to get your head around; an institutional antipathy towards the mentally ill.

Before I made my claim, I was told by fellow sufferers and advisers on an OCD charity forum, that I should be able to claim two types of benefit with my condition: Personal Independence Payment(PIP) and Employment Support Allowance(ESA). It was eventually made clear to me that the government had just changed the rules to prevent people with OCD from getting PIP. I was already well into the application process and I disagreed with this change on general principle. So I pursued it regardless, going through the motions of appealing and eventually attending a tribunal. There was never much hope though, and as expected, I was turned down for PIP. So I concentrated my efforts on my application for ESA, which is supposed to be the UK's basic benefit provision for people who are unemployed due to ill health. I had previously been given the impression that this claim would be a formality with a diagnosis of OCD. Boy oh boy, was I ever wrong.

Apparently it was not enough that I'd merely been subjected to the crushing pressure of losing my job in my forties, battling an undiagnosed severe mental health condition for decades, watching my savings disappear in the face of long-term unemployment, and increasingly having to care for my ageing parents, including an abusive father who made that task as difficult as humanly possible. Oh no, according to the Department of Work and Pensions(DWP: the UK's welfare services), I also needed to be subjected to a vicious year-long siege upon my psyche, comprising convoluted forms, intrusive assessments, mendacious rejections which I had to appeal against, and finally a terrifying tribunal hearing. All of which had to be duplicated for the two benefits I'd claimed for - PIP and ESA. And all of which had to be duplicated all over again with the Citizens Advice Bureau(CAB) as well as the DWP. "But why?" you may well ask. Well I'll tell you why: because I was reliably informed prior to the process, that the system was secretly rigged so that unless you enlisted third party assistance from someone like the CAB, then your claim was refused right off the bat, completely regardless of the contents of your form. The phrase "kangaroo court" springs to mind.

As an OCD sufferer, the worst aspect of this process, was the deliberate deceit on the part of the DWP. Throughout every single part of the process, they pretended that they knew absolutely nothing about OCD. So it was up to me to repeatedly explain it from scratch every step of the way - filling in the form, having the assessment, when I appealed, and when I had the tribunal. And every single time, the next person in the chain pointedly hadn't read anything from the previous interactions in the process, and claimed to know nothing about OCD. It's like a form of military interrogation or psychological torture. It really feels like they're trying to provoke a negative response so that they can make it about that instead, and invalidate your claim.

I find it incredibly hard to believe that I was the first person they'd ever seen with pure O, let alone with OCD. Yet that is how they consistently acted throughout my dealings with them. I can't help but think it's a deliberate strategy designed to create an air of bewildered ignorance and convenient misunderstanding. Thus obfuscating the proceedings, wearing down the claimant, and decreasing their chances of making a convincing case. Either way it will certainly make them reluctant to put themselves through such a traumatising process a second time.

When the DWP rejects your claim for ESA, you can appeal against the decision, but it takes many weeks for that to be processed. In the meantime they automatically switch you to another benefit called Job Seeker's Allowance(JSA) which is the benefit that healthy unemployed people get. Once you're on JSA, the DWP has carte blanche to ignore your health problems, and badger you mercilessly until you take voluntary or paid work. Now when they're rejecting every legitimate ESA claim by default, this part of the process smacks of a cynically transparent "Catch-22" ruse designed to bully unwell people into working before they even get a chance to appeal their ESA decision. It's a very dehumanising experience to go through and it had a terrible effect on my OCD.

When my claim for ESA was rejected, they sent a report justifying their decision. This report conspicuously ignored every single scrap of pertinent evidence which I'd provided in support of my claim, both on the form and during the assessment. Instead they cherry-picked the information I'd provided, to clumsily try and paint a picture of someone unafflicted by OCD, who had fraudulently claimed benefits which they weren't entitled to. Anyone who knows anything about OCD will know that wrongly accusing an OCD sufferer of something they didn't do is huge no-no. It preys upon your problems around certainty and scrupulosity. It forces you to mercilessly revisit a situation you were previously sure about, revalidating what really happened and what did not, until the doubt goes away again. But of course that relief is only temporary, and before you know it, you're saddled with a new obsession/compulsion pairing to add to your menagerie. The obsessions and compulsions I was left with as a result of their implicit accusations had a dramatically bad effect on my mental health during that year and for a long time thereafter. You end up in a very unpleasant cycle of alternating dread and trauma for the duration of your claim, and of course even worse dread if the cycle repeats the following year.

In response to all of this, I had to abandon the steps I was taking to try and improve my situation and, in effect, become my own legal defence for the duration of the claims process. I had to miss my brother's fiftieth birthday celebration to prepare my case the night before the tribunal. I found myself trapped in the throes of a long, drawn-out, acrimonious legal battle, just to apply for a basic benefit which didn't even cover my rent; a benefit which I should have been entitled to anyway, no questions asked, having previously been diagnosed with OCD.

How can this be the standard welfare assessment process for a citizen with a crippling mental health condition in a supposedly civilised country like Great Britain in the twenty-first century? A condition which, by definition, is exacerbated by stressful ordeals and false accusations of dishonesty. Clearly it is grotesquely inappropriate, and only serves to aggravate the very problem that delivered the claimant into the hands of the welfare services in the first place. It is so diametrically opposed to what the OCD sufferer actually needs in that situation, that I believe there ought to be a criminal investigation into its conception.

This ordeal moved me to write a long email to the (then) Prime Minister, David Cameron. I copied in all the members of his cabinet whose emails I could locate, including the Health Secretary, Jeremy Hunt, and soon-to-be Prime Minister Theresa May. I also copied in the leader of the opposition, Jeremy Corbyn, and pertinent members of his shadow cabinet. Yet not a single one of these very handsomely paid elected representatives had the professionalism or common decency to respond to me, despite my re-sending the email twice and requesting an explanation as to why nobody had replied.

Throughout my year long nightmare, one thing that was consistently used against me every single step of the way, was the fact that I was not taking SSRI medication. This, despite the fact that I'd made it abundantly clear why from the get-go; in the forms, assessments, appeal letters; all the way through to the tribunals. Regardless, all of the key players in this process attempted to wield this fact as some kind of smoking gun evidence that I didn't really have OCD, or that my OCD couldn't be taken seriously because medication wasn't involved. This is incredibly flawed backward thinking with no grounding in reality. It smacks of convenient sophistry invoked for all the wrong reasons.

As a result of all the thinly-veiled accusations of dishonesty levelled at me by the DWP, my progress in therapy was completely derailed and my OCD worsened considerably. It became crystal clear to me, that it's a waste of time trying to take on therapy if you're at the mercy of these people. ERP is already a tricky "two steps forward, one step back" kind of deal. But under these circumstances, it becomes a hopeless dance of "one step forward, twenty steps back". It's just too damned hard to make those precious gains, only to see them washed away again overnight thanks to someone else's deliberate pre-meditated incompetence.

Ultimately, after a surprisingly unpleasant tribunal where I was hectored from the moment I set foot in the room by the presiding judge and the appointed "medical professional", I succeeded in getting my claim for ESA upheld for twelve months. Alas, I don't think their decision was born out of any sudden new-found feelings of compassion. I think it rather more likely that they begrudgingly upheld my appeal because I brought up a technicality that they couldn't wriggle out of.

Tired of playing the performing monkey for blind-folded shills acting out a foregone conclusion, I decided I couldn't face going through this process again. So I was determined to try and use that year to turn my life around. Apparently the DWP didn't think I'd quite suffered enough though, and no sooner had the tribunal ended, than they started harassing me again, demanding that I fill out new assessment forms and attend new assessments. This happened twice in succession, and I had a hell of a run-around trying to convince them that I'd just been through the process and had my claim upheld. A clear pattern had emerged that left me wondering if I was being deliberately persecuted by these people. Again, this was rich fuel for OCD.

I've tried so hard to use the last twelve months wisely, but fate has not been on my side. My parents have had serious back-to-back health problems which have dominated the year and taken up a surprising amount of my time. That, together with my ever-increasing care commitments at home, have made it very tough making any solid progress with anything to improve my situation. I've continued to apply for work along the way, in hope that a job might remove the dread of having to deal with the DWP again. However, I face a wall of recruitment consultants who control the IT job market now in the UK. They won't even give me a shot at junior positions in the field I used to work in. It doesn't matter how I word my CV or the covering letters. No one will give me a look in. I've tried for lots of jobs where there seems to be a skills cross-over, and it's exactly the same story. Most people don't bother replying to my applications. I feel like I've become persona non grata and my career is over. That's very hard to swallow after investing so many years of hard work into what I thought would be a lifelong career.

Of course, were I to get a job, I have every reason to expect that I'd end up in exactly the same place I was in five years ago, when I had to take a break after redundancy, because I was completely burned out from OCD. But it's either that or be at the mercy of these charlatans for a pittance I can't live on anyway. So it comes down to the lesser of two evils. And that is how they wriggle out of their responsibility unfortunately. That is how they win.

I've been living in a state of slowly mounting dread for the last twelve months as this process has drawn closer. It's like a nightmare to me that I have to go through it again despite the promise I made myself a year ago. My OCD is already through the roof, catastrophising through all the permutations. My thoughts turn to all my mentally ill brothers and sisters throughout the UK who have had to face this torment, completely unequipped to deal with it. You get a taste of the spiralling dread that pushed so many of them over the edge. My heart goes out to those poor souls and their families left behind. This shameful persecution of the mentally ill citizens of Great Britain by their own government is long past its expiry date. It's time that it was stamped out for good, and those responsible were held accountable.

Let me just re-iterate how these tacit assumptions about CBT and SSRI medication were manipulated against me throughout this process; to paint a false picture of a fraudulent claimant who either couldn't be bothered taking advantage of an available cure, or who didn't really have OCD in the first place. Either way, I was not taken seriously and had to fight viciously to defend my corner throughout the process.

As stated previously, I'm not qualified in medicine or therapy or pharmacology. So this is all nothing more than the conjecture and personal opinion of a layman. However, I am somebody who's lived with OCD all of his life; someone who's read about OCD and conversed with an awful lot of fellow sufferers; someone who's tried the SSRIs; someone who's tried the therapy; someone who's come out of the other end uncured; someone who now has to explain himself to everyone around him because they've been conditioned to view that through a lens of failure. So I feel like I've paid my dues enough to be allowed to have an opinion on these things. Yet, challenging any of these tacit assumptions on OCD forums, in a doctor's surgery, in therapy, or when interfacing with the government, very quickly results in reprimand, ridicule, financial penalty, censorship, or being ostracised from the group.

I don't think this draconian censorship or these flawed assumptions are anywhere near reconcilable with such a recently discovered and barely understood phenomenon. As sufferers, I think we should be allowed to disagree with these assumptions, and discuss our disorder freely without being chaperoned, reprimanded or penalised. Ultimately, it should be our sovereign right to choose whether or not we wish to take medication, and that choice should be respected thereafter by all parties concerned. I think we need to guard against governments and private interests who would happily exploit our disorder for financial gain. Crucially, I think all citizens need to start scrutinising and challenging the dubious relationship that's evolved between their governments and the pharmaceutical and private healthcare industries. Moreover, we should all avoid drinking the Kool-aid and becoming polarised into combatants in someone else's battle. Instead, working together, we should try to keep open minds until such a time as we're truly sure about the nature of this disorder and how it might be best treated.

I thought it important to make it clear how I feel about these subjects since some of my poems reflect these contentious views. I know these opinions are going against the grain and I don't expect to get any love for them, but I wouldn't be doing my principles or my experience of OCD any justice if I were to censor them to please the crowd. I do however accept that my opinions could be misguided or wrong. All that I ask the reader to do is to accept that theirs could be too, and to try to keep an open mind. It is only with open minds, uncensored discussion, and untainted scientific endeavour, that this most cruel and unusual phenomenon will one day be understood and truly cured. Surely that ought to be the collective goal for all sufferers and non-sufferers alike.

A note on the title:

The idiom "Drinking the Kool-aid" harks back to the tragic events that unfolded on 18th November 1978, in Jonestown, Guyana. Often misleadingly referred to as The Jonestown Massacre, this incident saw over nine hundred members of an American cult called The People's Temple take their own lives by drinking Kool-aid laced with cyanide.

Their charismatic cult leader, Jim Jones, coerced them into taking this drastic action shortly before shooting himself. The spurious arguments Jones used to persuade them, belied his secret desperation to avoid being imminently exposed for orchestrating murders within the cult, and for indulging in forbidden sexual relations with cult members.

In more recent times, the term has become synonymous with blindly buying into dubious ideas under duress.

Thank You

Thank you very much for choosing my book and taking the time to read it.

If you enjoyed it, I'd really appreciate a review on Amazon.

If you didn't enjoy it, I'd really appreciate a review on Trip Advisor. (Sorry - I couldn't resist)

Why not join my mailing list for news about forthcoming releases: www.sjellico.wordpress.com

I promise I won't send spam or pass your details onto anyone else. On the same website, you can read some more about me, along with poems, news, and updates about what I'm working on.

I did the editing and proof reading for this book myself so there's every chance I've missed the odd typo or spelling mistake. If you happen to have noticed anything along the way, then I'd be most grateful if you'd drop me a line and let me know: sherwynjellico@gmail.com

This book would be nothing but forgotten words without you picking it up and giving meaning to them. Thank you so much.

Acknowledgements

I would like to thank the following people for their kindness, support and encouragement during the making of this book(in reverse order of how long I've known you - a transparent and shameful ruse to dodge the inevitable favouritism quagmire):

My amazing mother who has been an unfailing star in the bleakest of nights. A debt I could never repay and would never be expected to.

My brother for shooting the breeze over the cover, the title and the message.

Rob for persisting in pouring water onto stone and remaining a friend through the worst of times.

My niece for her scarily insightful feedback on the cover design.

Tricia for having the courage to go against the grain in the lion's den. More power to you!

Abby and Deborah in The Netherlands for their Dutch courage and positive can-do vibes.

Tracy for creative sound boarding, encouragement, and laughing at my bad(great) jokes.

Nela for somehow soldiering through my entire back catalogue of poems and leaving lovely comments on each and every one of them. Hvala ti Nela!

Khadeja for demonstrating the power of positivity in the face of formidable adversity.

Morgaine for lending a kind ear through tough times and for showing me there's still faery magick to be found in this wicked world.

Lynne, Irina and Susan for your friendship and kind poetry feedback.

Finally, I'd like to thank Paulo Ordoveza for allowing me to quote his elegant definition of the phrase "Begging the question" at the start of this book. Please visit Paulo's website for a full disambiguation of this oft-misused phrase:
www.begthequestion.info

www.ingramcontent.com/pod-product-compliance
Lightning Source LLC
Chambersburg PA
CBHW071551030726
47593CB00001BA/108